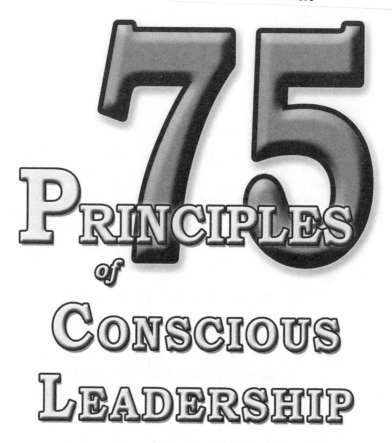

75 PRINCIPLES of CONSCIOUS LEADERSHIP

Inspired Skills for 21st Century Business

Michael Schantz

Robert D. Reed Publishers • Bandon, OR

Robert D. Reed Publishers
P.O. Box 1992
Bandon, OR 97411
Phone: 541-347-9882 • Fax: -9883
E-mail: 4bobreed@msn.com
web site: www.rdrpublishers.com

Editors: **Maureen Kinsey, Barbara Harrison,
        Cleone Lyvonne**
Cover Designer: **Cleone Lyvonne**
Typesetter: **Barbara Kruger**

ISBN: 978-1-934759-06-6
ISBN 10: 1-934759-06-6

Library of Congress Control Number 2007943461

Manufactured, Typeset and Printed in the United States of America

Dedication

I dedicate this book, with love and gratitude, to the people who have contributed so much to my life:

- My dear parents, Edith and Joseph, who launched me on this exciting journey;

- Ammachi, my beloved teacher, known to many as the "hugging saint," a living beacon of inspiration, compassion, and nurturing for the world;

- Steve Chandler, my legendary coach, whose work, inspiration and example helped awaken this book within me;

- Steve D'Annunzio, a mentor and author, whose enthusiasm, humor, and brilliance are immeasurable;

- Drs. Ron and Mary Hulnick, psychologists and master educators of the University of Santa Monica, for their experiential programs in healing, spirituality, and leadership;

- Hal Rose, my first coach and great friend, who embodies leadership in every moment and action;

- Byron Katie, who has given the world a new light with *The Work*; and

- Marisa, who has always unconditionally believed in me with her quintessential Italian heart.

A Vision for the 21st Century Organization

For institutional solvency now hinges upon the ability to restructure along the vibrational lines of the intensifying energy field of awakening consciousness, in patterns compatible with (the) diverse forms that love can take. Not only will this assure their (institutions') survival, but more important, it will assist the overall human transition from the *fear-dominated* historical order to the new order of *love-centered* creation. Their skill at this, and the degree of consciousness with which they participate, will determine the level of their prosperity.

—Ken Carey
Author of *The Third Millennium*

Contents

Foreword

As an executive mentor, workshop presenter, and avid reader of personal-development material since 1975, it is rare these days to read something truly original in our field of endeavor. I can tell you that this book is an ego-less work that authentically cites all its sources, and yet takes them one step further. True teachers deeply feel the responsibility to add some fresh insight that takes ancient truth and makes it usable it for the business leader. Originality and insight are the important qualities that define greatness.

If you were to study the work of the greats, you would notice a powerful flashpoint that occurred in each of their lives. There came a time when they had done the requisite amount of life work to the degree at which they left their teacher's style behind and began to develop their own. This is the way of things with all true student/teachers. It occurs only when the crucible of life has forged the student through the perfect blend of pain, joy, sickness, healing, life, death, togetherness, loneliness, depression, and ecstasy. Only then is one ready to access and download special insights from the infinite, and to teach and write. One must pay one's dues to earn the ability to teach and write from what is truly, and I say this with the utmost reverence, the spiritual. Michael Schantz has paid these dues, as the material you are about to read will reveal.

Through the many hours Michael and I have since spent traversing the universe on a variety of topics, I can wholeheartedly tell you the following. Few people I know have spent as much time studying, meditating on, and applying the teachings of universal laws and mind as Michael has. Michael is quite possibly the most well-read man I have ever met, but more than that, he applies what he has learned from the great teachers in a way that uplifts the world. His love of truth is as admirable as his ability to write it. Far from being a man who can just speak principles, he is also a very successful entrepreneur in his own right; which means *he lives it.*

In my last book, I outlined five levels of entrepreneurs I had worked with in my thirty years as a life-success coach/productivity trainer. Those five levels are, from lowest to highest productivity; fear-driven, desire-driven, pride-driven, mission-driven, and love-driven. The love-driven beings are a rare and precious resource, as love-driven people make up only 4% of the population in the world and .01% in the business world. Michael is in that .01%.

You are holding a precious resource on leadership in your hands. It is a treatise on personal, entrepreneurial, and spiritual leadership principles that contain contemporary insight that I never before have seen in print. Please commit to reading and finishing this book, and have a highlighter handy to capture its many gems for quick reference later on. You will find this work to contain a unique combination of powerful principles, while retaining a lightness that makes it eminently readable.

May you enjoy it as much as I did.

—Steve D'Annunzio
Rochester, NY

Preface

Reading Michael Schantz's brilliant *75 Principles of Conscious Leadership* causes the reader to be swung between two polarities of thought: first, "This is way ahead of its time!" and second, "I hope he's not too late—it should have been written years ago."

Michael Schantz has done the world a huge and everlasting service. He's digested and explained the very best writing on leadership and consciousness and made it accessible to us all. From the complex cosmic work of Ken Wilber to the timeless epiphanies of Ralph Waldo Emerson, this book has taken organizations into a conscious realm that no other leadership work has attempted.

That it succeeds is the good part. It's the fun part, because Michael has made a conscious, spiritual approach to leadership wonderfully practical. He's brought it into the workplace in such a bold and graceful way that it may never leave. And by infusing the book with his own unabashed personal stories, he gives us life by sharing his. Conscious leadership is not some new age, goofy "spirituality" but the real thing: the very same thing that the greatest leaders of all time used to lead mankind, countries, and companies.

The beauty of this book is in its multitude of well-researched resources. All the most powerful leadership thinkers are here in a newly understandable format. Now we get the whole picture. It would take a single individual many years, if not decades, to bring all this diverse insight under one cover. Michael has offered his life up to leaders, spiritual guides and mentors with courageous vulnerability. His openness to being influenced is the book's supreme gift to the reader. The humble credit he gives throughout to those whose ideas and practices have influenced him paradoxically makes both him and the book that much stronger. He has given his life to this work.

Especially useful are the Principles: short, colorful, and powerful. These are the essence of the full transformation to becoming and being a leader. Then, when you read his last chapter on the levels of consciousness from which a leader operates, you will know where you are right now! But the real beauty of this book is that you will also feel the transformation that is happening to you with practice of the skills and transition to the next level. Can a book really do that? Read it and see.

—Steve Chandler
Phoenix, AZ

Prologue

This book came into being as my response to a deep calling within me. My intention became to create one volume that contained the very best of the principles, practices and skills of conscious leadership for the leaders of the 21st Century organization. I distilled the learning from my personal coaching, my studies in leadership, spirituality and psychology, my mastermind group, plus many years of professional management, experience, and observation. Then, I prepared by reading many other respected authors on leadership, organizations, and consciousness.

75 Principles of Conscious Leadership is a compendium of the conscious skills of leadership, human communication, human motivation, and mentoring. This book is a manual, or handbook, of time-honored disciplines of effective communication and spiritual consciousness, foundational to leadership as a life's practice. Woven through all of the principles are the qualities of compassion, service, contribution and loving, positive regard.

As the book portrays, the principles and practices of leadership comprise a discipline, a lifelong experience through continual refinement. Learning leadership, effectively, requires commitment, as all transformation starts from within. The principles of conscious leadership are available to anyone who embraces them and incorporates them into their professional lives and their personal relationships.

The answer, I am convinced, is that they are among us. Out there in the settings with which we are all familiar are the unawakened leaders, feeling no overpowering call to lead and hardly aware of the potential within.... How do you send out a call to the unawakened leaders? How do you make them aware of their leadership potential? How do you make leadership feasible and tolerable for leaders? ... It is my belief that with some imagination and social inventiveness we could tap these hidden reserves—not just for government, not just for business, but for the diverse leadership needs of a dynamic society.

—John Gardner
Founder of Common Cause,
Stanford University Professor

It is my sincere desire that this book assists you in awakening the leadership skills, which already live within you. With blessings and inspiration for your journey of leadership and leadership consciousness,

Michael Schantz
Los Angeles, CA

Principle 1

Embrace Leadership as a Learned Discipline

But, leadership is not that easy. We con ourselves into believing that the word is the same as the action. The ability to lead doesn't come from a snappy vocabulary, the books you've displayed on your shelves, your place on the organizational chart, or that fashionable title on your business card. Leadership is always substantive and rarely fashionable. It is intensely personal and intrinsically scary, and it requires us to live the ideas we espouse—in irrefutable ways—every day of our lives, up to and beyond the point of fear.

—Steve Farber
Author of *The Radical Leap*

Leadership is about inspiration—of oneself and of others. Great leadership is about human experiences, not processes. Leadership is not a formula or a program, it is a human activity that comes from the heart and considers the heart of others.

—Lance Secretan
Author and teacher

Leaders understand that genuine leadership is not a style, an idiom, or a destination. They define and embrace leadership as a committed, continuous refining *process*. Effective leaders engage their role as action; leadership to them is a verb and not a noun.

Steve Farber assigns leadership the nickname of "an extreme sport." These are great words and a very fitting analogy. Great athletes envision, practice, and focus. They practice continually to ultimately play and perform as fully committed and engaged. Leaders adopt this athletic approach to leading, learning, and improving leadership as a practice, a continual discipline.

The familiar approaches to leading—such as management by objective, quality circles, down or right sizing, thinking outside-of-the-box, market penetration, financial re-engineering or creative accounting, reconfiguring the organizational chart, distribution system management, or systems change—only address certain short-term objectives while they create many new issues.

Leadership can always be recognized as a presence. Leaders live the process with energy and zeal. They have moved beyond the boundaries of success and acquisition into the search for a larger, more satisfying life experience, one of contribution. Vigorous leadership is built on the twin core elements of personal evolved humanity. Leadership comes from a lifetime of learning. Embrace leadership as a learned discipline.

Principle 2

Lead as a Master Servant

Control is not leadership, management is not leadership, leadership is leadership. If you don't know that you work for your mislabeled 'subordinates,' then you know nothing of leadership; you only know tyranny.

—Dee Hock
Chairman Emeritus, Visa International

If our economic organizations are going to live up to their potential, we must find, develop and encourage more people to lead in the service of others. Without leadership, firms cannot adapt to a fast moving world. But if leaders do not have the heart of service, there is only the potential for tyranny.

—John Kotter
Harvard Business School

The typical structure of an organization, its pyramid, was designed and functioned to ultimately serve the leader and the interests of the stakeholders.

A new approach to leading would be to invert the pyramid, literally turn the organizational chart upside-down.

The inverted pyramid would then appear with the organization's clients forming the apex, the employees comprising the center, and the leader holding the base of the pyramid.

In this new leadership model, the leader literally forms the foundation of the entire organization, and all aspects of the organization are designed to move upward toward the clients with superior service. This cutting-edge leadership/organizational model has been termed the Aggregate System approach to leadership.

As leaders embrace service to clients as the pinnacle, the foundation for the organization, work for the optimal good of everyone moves throughout the entire organization. The result is that the service then flows from the leader through the employees directly to clients.

Everyone serves and receives service, thus everyone benefits toward the good of all. An effective leader leads as a master servant for all stakeholders.

Principle 3

Create an Integrated Vision and Mission Statement

I will devote a disproportionate amount of time to creating a corporate environment where the company's guiding principles are clearly stated, heard and practiced— where employees hold each other accountable to practice these statements.

—Bill Lyons
CEO, American Century

So, it's my primary job as a motivator to create a vision of who we want to be, and then live in that picture as if it were already happening in this very moment.

—Steve Chandler
Author of *100 Ways to Motivate Others*

The company vision statement expresses the beliefs of an organization or business relationship, and a mission statement details the reasons the organization exists. The vision addresses what an organization does, and the mission addresses the motivation, shared values, and core beliefs of the stakeholders.

The vision and mission statements contain the entire *purpose* of the organization. Ideally, they define and answer the culture and direction of the organization. They guide and direct employees to understand what they accomplish during their workdays.

The vision describes the products or services the organization wishes to provide. It uses consensus to identify core business lines and the overall purpose of the business. The mission delineates the purpose and reason that the organization creates products or services and explains why creating these products and services is important.

The mission serves as the base for strategic and tactical planning and distills how the organization will thrive and grow. It informs outside stakeholders (such as customers or clients, lenders, shareholders, and suppliers) the business of the organization and the means to achieve success and excellence in its endeavor. The mission communicates the needs the organization meets and whom the organization serves.

In the new paradigm of conscious leadership, an integrated organization will create a vision and mission statement that encompasses aspects of the physical, the mental, the emotional, and the ethical/spiritual levels of the human family.

For the conscious organization, the physical level provides the structure for the endeavor of the enterprise; the mental level provides a foundation for decision making and manifesting goals and objectives; the emotional level engenders meaning and pride in people; and the ethical/spiritual level provides clarity of purpose to align with the core values and ethics of the organization, its leaders, and employees.

When an organization incorporates and implements these aspects in its vision and mission, the leader and employees will have created a comprehensive blueprint for conscious relationships. Its purpose, beliefs, and values will clearly reflect a new encompassing spiritual application to business. This integrated vision and mission statements emanate from the core purpose of the organization and its values. With a well-defined mission and vision statement, leadership has a strong foundation upon which to build the company culture and focus its growth over time.

Principle 4

Access and Trust
Authentic Intuition

Adversity doesn't build character, it reveals it.

—Anonymous

A leader assumes the role of a pioneer and often navigates unknown regions. A leader must often make decisions where no precedent, research, or available statistical history exist. Exploring emerging markets, where new state-of-the-art products and services are created, serves as one example of this decision-making.

Although most of us have heard the expression "trust your gut," there is often great value received by "attuning" to intuition. It is a form of indistinct, higher knowledge, which becomes present at times.

Intuition may be reliably called upon to play a part in the important role of decision-making. A leader aligns with higher wisdom through intuition. While some leaders may scoff at the notion of using intuition because there is no hard science to prove results, many renowned and innovative leaders know and use intuition frequently. Many have heard an inner voice, a guide, advising whether or not to proceed. Great inventors, artists, musicians, and teachers throughout history have readily acknowledged higher guidance.

Intuition derived from that inner world of knowing originates in an outside source. Rupert Sheldrake, a British physicist, identified energy fields that surround our bodies and form a field of knowing, or intuition. Many leaders have relied on information and instinct to make informed decisions. Conscious intuition has become a trusted aspect of the decision-making process as new business paradigms emerge.

Ken Wilbur, a systems and organizational philosopher, suggests that an order of the highest purpose and certitude emerges from apparent chaos. He is one of the forward-thinking visionaries who observes advanced, emerging states of being. The entire theory of Spiral Dynamics embraces the vision that human knowledge is continually expanding in an evolutionary fashion. The dynamic evolves upward, ever expanding, and transcending present knowledge. It follows then that our recognition of and access to emerging knowledge would do the same. Embrace intuition as a conscious leadership skill.

Principle 5

Embrace Risk in Decision-Making

A life spent making mistakes is not only more honorable but more useful than a life spent doing nothing.
—George Bernard Shaw
Irish writer

You've got to be willing to take a risk. (It's) very easy to say but in business— especially—very hard to do. The irony is, risk is a very natural part of the human experience and we accept it in many areas of our lives without realizing it. But a lot of business people who call themselves leaders want things to be easy and painless. They're either kidding themselves or lying.
—Steve Farber

Leaders make decisions within complex systems involving many parameters. Often, at inception, the variables of decisions are unclear and multifaceted in scope. It is natural to experience emotional response to the unknown.

When uncertainty arises, leaders may feel out of their comfort zone. However, uncertainty is often a leader's best indicator that new information, the not-yet known, may be present. Instead of shrinking from risk-related fear or avoiding discomfort, the leader has another choice. The leader chooses mind shift and learning.

The leader can transcend uncertainty and navigate through vagaries by embracing risk rather than avoiding it. Fear can serve as a resource of learning for leaders who use it to their advantage. Fear is often the precursor to some new, unexplored possibility and may be interpreted as excitement for the new, not-yet known.

The ability to integrate fear inherent within risk is crucial for leaders in all dimensions of life. If fear is interpreted as excitement, it serves the leader as motivation for learning and exploration within the decision-making process.

Principle 6

Listen Exquisitely by Using Perception Checking

The ear of the leader must ring with the voices of the people.

—Woodrow Wilson

We should never pretend to know what we don't know, we should not feel ashamed to ask and learn from people below, and we should listen carefully to the views of the cadres at the lowest levels. Be a pupil before you become a teacher; learn from the cadres at the lower levels before you issue orders.

—Mao Tse-tung

In my experience, exquisite listening promotes effective communication and lets people know that they are being heard with your attentive, focused interest. Perception checking offers a dual benefit. It clarifies dialogue and it also informs the speakers that you care about their information. You listen for accuracy and for deep understanding.

When presenting an issue, challenge or question after the speaker has finished or paused, you might respond by saying: *"What I heard you say was ____, meaning that ____. Is that accurate?"* or *"If I heard you correctly, then you are expressing ____. Is this correct?"*

or "*Great, so let's see if I understand correctly. I believe you expressed to me* _____. *Is mine an accurate depiction?*"

In the rapid, hectic pace of business, leaders and employees often do not fully engage or listen. Individuals often formulate a response before the speaker has completed speaking or, even worse, interrupt and finish their dialogue.

This belittles the speaker and inhibits the flow and exchange of information. In this environment, the speaker's unique contribution and perspective may never be shared or heard.

Opportunities are lost and many misunderstandings and errors occur in today's business world through poor listening. Faulty communication and lackluster listening in business contribute to poor planning and ineffective service and execution. Poor listening erodes team building and responsible sharing.

An effective leader creates an environment where connection is understood, appreciated, and encouraged. Here contributions are welcome and true relationships are formed that serve clients and afford all individuals an opportunity to motivate, express, and enjoy themselves.

Principle 7

Give People Your Time and Full Attention

Most of the successful people I've known are the ones who do more listening than talking.
—Bernard Baruch, statesman and financier
Presidential Advisor, WWI and WWII

You cannot truly listen to anyone and do anything else at the same time.
—M. Scott Peck (1936-2005)
Author of *The Road Less Traveled*

In his workshop *"The Focused Leader,"* Steve Chandler identifies how people subtly sabotage business relationships when they do not extend people sufficient time and their undivided attention. As a result, people diminish and devalue each other in business relationships. When people take other phone calls, glance at e-mails, or cut allotted time for meetings, they send a loud albeit often unintended message that "other things are more important than *you* are." Not affording people due consideration and respect can be toxic to business relationships.

Research suggests that sixty-five percent of respondents directly attribute job satisfaction to an effective relationship with their immediate superior. Just imagine the implications and the impact on business relationships when leaders do not treat employees on their teams with professional consideration and due respect. Business relationships erode when people are not nurtured and their skills are not developed and honored by leaders. Individuals experience an inability to contribute and they do not feel valued.

Chandler demonstrates that rushing communication to save management time is counterproductive. Hurrying erodes business relationships. He makes a strong case that investing even thirty minutes of "quality" time with an employee may ultimately save hours of maintenance to repair and restore an ailing relationship.

Effective leaders need to recognize, acknowledge, and develop employees so that they grow and hone their skills. Leaders must actively communicate that ideas are welcome and vital to them, for the greater success of the organization, business relationships, and the clients.

Communicative leaders serve as a superb example when they remain flexible, welcome ideas, offer quality time, and listen with genuine interest and complete attention to their team and the company's clients.

Principle 8

Set Priorities Wisely

The key is not to prioritize what's on your schedule, but to schedule your priorities.
—Stephen R. Covey

This skill combines the time-honored maxims: "If it's worth doing, it's worth doing well;" and "If it's a worthwhile endeavor, then the endeavor deserves adequate time and effort." In business, deadlines are there for a reason; they propel action.

A precept of the time-management classic book entitled "The Time Trap," a left-brain approach separates matters that *seemed urgent* from those that were *genuinely important.*

In his practical book *Getting Things Done*, business consultant David Allen expands priority setting. David refines priority setting and elevates it sequentially into levels and actions.

He orders and then ranks priorities in a unique multi-tier system that allows people to "stop renting out their minds to their schedule." He decries constant re-jockeying of priorities and changing of schedules, and he espouses intentionally and purposefully performing desired tasks. People work better in empowered and self-determined priority systems where they maintain their own focus and clarity.

What David proposes is a continuum from "high priority/must do immediately" all the way to a "no urgency/get to it later." However, an integrated system needs to be devised to divide tasks into the designated categories. His mission is to give workers freedom and peace of mind in the workplace with this system. Rather than using precious energy worrying about tasks and thinking about unassigned priorities, once tasks are prioritized, then organized into a system, the mind is free.

David Allen and a number of leadership authors explain that people waste time and expend precious energy when they continually reshuffle deliverables and approach prioritizing tasks using their minds, rather than a dependable system. When individuals choose an integrated right-brain approach, they use applied intelligence and energy to complete tasks and achieve goals one by one.

Leaders and employees can more effectively commit their resources and full attention to completing one task at a time and meeting "high priority" goals when they set priorities from their right brains. Using this expanded approach results in successful outcomes for leaders, employees, and clients.

Principle 9

Choose Unconditional Positive Regard

Treat a man as he is and he will remain as he is; treat a man as he can be and should be, and he will become as he can be and should be.

—Goethe
German poet

Carl Rogers, the renowned psychologist and co-founder of the human potential movement, often stated that unconditional positive regard is a foundation of effective human communication and interaction. Participants feel encouraged to bond and find common ground with each other. Choosing unwavering positive regard to all individuals is a conscious action. The "unconditional" application means that people approach all situations and matters with positive regard without exception. Unconditional positive regard creates a positive environment and supports positive relationships.

Individuals sense, appreciate, and often reciprocate when you approach them from a place of positive regard. People know on a tangible level, through intuition, when they are afforded respect and consideration. When leaders extend genuine interest, people most often respond in kind. With positive regard, respect is built into company relationships.

Like a magnet, positive regard attracts more of itself and elicits positive responses. That respect reinforces effective communication.

Leaders will find that employees and clients respond favorably when leaders express genuine caring and take an active interest in their interactions. Employees naturally feel more comfortable and readily share their ideas and themselves with a leader who values them and extends positive regard. When individuals feel valued and esteemed, they are encouraged to communicate and work enthusiastically.

Over time, unconditional positive regard becomes an integral part of the company culture and communication style. It embodies meaningful connection through caring communication and mutual respect. In my experience as a business leader, I have found nothing more important to effective human communication and interaction than choosing positive regard and listening with genuine interest.

Principle 10

Perform Key Objectives One by One

The older I get, the more wisdom I find in the ancient rule of taking first things first; a process which often reduces the most complex human problem to manageable proportion.

—Dwight D. Eisenhower
General and president

Effective managers do first things first, and they do one thing at a time.

—Peter Drucker
Global business consultant

I know a number of skilled leaders and coaches who teach that people actually get more done by slowing down rather than stressing out on multiple priorities. Slowing down and focusing preserve the natural energy flow and assist the mind in task completion. A number of consultants emphasize that people use more energy as they distract themselves because they lose focus and become frustrated by stress and confusion. Stress, confusion, and unfocused work drain energy as people lose momentum. And nothing can de-motivate a worker faster than falling behind in goals.

Research suggests that multiple tasking is ineffective. People expend more energy working on multiple tasks. Individuals use less energy if they complete tasks on a one-by-one basis. On its surface, this approach may seem too simple. Leaders and employees may choose to try this approach and set aside the multitasking approach for one day per week, and then compare the results.

Research also demonstrates that multitasking increases stress because worry sets in when focused achievement is lost. From experience, I view multitasking as a myth. It sounds good in theory but does not work well in practice. People accomplish more when they focus and discourage or eliminate interruptions. When workers utilize their time and energy to complete single deliverables, they finish work tasks in a structured order. The focus and completion feel rewarding as tasks are accomplished.

Although practicing this one-task approach may prove to be a challenge in the technology-bombarded business culture, I encourage you to try it. Unplug and determine if you have completed more tasks with less stress. Individuals can move away from their current sound-byte mode and return to providing quality work product and optimal work flow through an energized pace and orderly, structured work flow.

Principle 11

Eliminate Anxiety

Our anxiety does not empty tomorrow of its sorrows, but only empties today of its strength.

—Charles H. Spurgeon
19th Century Theologian

Being overwhelmed is not solely a response to outside stimuli and circumstances. From a conscious perspective, being overwhelmed is a negatively focused future fantasy. People shift their focus from the present endeavor to the future, with negativity. The experience of being overwhelmed is a contemplation of imaginary catastrophe. The negativity comes from fear, a perceived lack of control over future events. By returning our focus to the present, we can positively influence the future with action steps in the present.

People can avoid becoming overwhelmed by remaining focused on present tasks and restraining thought about the future. From a conscious perspective, the future is created from the present. A powerful wisdom phrase that I embrace reads: "*The future is the source of all anxiety.*" Keeping our mind on the right path eliminates anxiety because action builds commitment and commitment builds confidence.

If my mind wanders and I ask, "How am I going to get all of this done on schedule?" I remember that the future is the source of anxiety. I quickly recognize that

I am sifting through the "future" clutter I created in my mind and return my thoughts to the present and perform the task at hand.

Many sociologists and psychologists believe that the need for constant activity and worry has become a near-addiction in our society. I attribute this compulsive behavior to guilt, when individuals believe that they must be productive in every moment. Endless doing erodes the sense of being. Steve Chandler also offers, "...this inability to be quiet is really just the inability to return the mind to the most important thing it can be thinking about in any given moment."

Individuals who grant themselves permission to slow down, can release anxiety and perform quality thinking. With quality thinking, individuals have the ability to examine other options, refine their thinking, and make new choices. Anxiety is toxic. Conscious leaders encourage individuals to eliminate anxiety, promote proactive behavior, and promulgate innovative ways of thinking and being.

Leaders may experiment to determine what works for them. My method is to write this process on an index card–it catches my eye and immediately returns me to the present time and task.

My "no anxiety" index card reads:

Set Clear Intention => Focus =>Plan time =>Achieve Results => Succeed!

Principle 12

Become a Self-Thinker

With differences come supreme teaching moments. Much learning is done in the face of adversity and mature leaders parsing and vetting options, choices, direction and strategy.

—Stephen R. Covey
Author of *Principle-Centered Leadership*

If you want to change how a person thinks, give up. You cannot change how another thinks. Give them a tool, the use of which will gradually lead them to think differently.

—Buckminster Fuller
Designer and architect

Some individuals in positions of leadership believe that they need to know more than anyone. They believe that they always need to know more than the people they lead. That opinion is disempowering and ineffective.

Learning is not gathering an ever-increasing volume of information. A renowned economics professor at The American University, Dr. Herbert Striner, taught me much beyond traditional learning.

He began his memorable lectures stating, "I am not here to teach you about economics; I am here to teach you how to *think* about economics." He really did challenge us to think for ourselves and encouraged us to ignore people's opinions about what we thought. Even though I did not fully appreciate it at the time, Dr. Striner was teaching us deep trust in our thinking.

Dr. Striner used to joke, "At the end of this course, I want you to have something more than another intelligent notebook." He wanted us to acquire and use thinking skills, rather than collect memorized information, most of which was forgotten several hours after the final exam.

Besides self-thinking, Dr. Striner encouraged and exemplified self-confidence. He took risks and held deep convictions. He truly inspired us, and we respected and appreciated the learning. He was both a true educator and an inspiring leader.

Dr. Striner also served on the Council of Economic Advisors for the U.S. president and served as dean of the American University's business school. Indeed, he exemplified the true leader in service who embodied the innate nature of education, that of self-thinking.

The word education finds its roots in *educare*, which translates as to "draw out." Learning to think for ourselves is self-empowering and leads to confidence in the process. The conscious approach to education is that of service through learning. Learned thinking for me is resourceful, confident, and self-reliant.

With regard to organizational leadership, Jim Collins, in *Good to Great*, says the organization that is continually learning, adopting, and refining best business practice to improve itself is the organization that *becomes* great. Conscious leaders who promote self-thinking and deep learning integrate a powerful resource into their organization. Self-thinking can become an integral part of the corporate culture where it is encouraged and supported.

Principle 13

Practice Empathy and Compassion

Leadership requires high levels of humanity. To be great leaders, we need to share our humanity and receive our people's humanity all day.

—Steve Chandler
Author of *Ten Commitments to Your Success*

The best definition I have ever heard states that "empathy is listening to another *as if* you were in their shoes, without losing the *as if* quality." This wisdom is profound. Empathy means we listen with full attention and offer people support with healthy boundaries so that we do not get "stuck" in their issue. The challenge or learning surrounding any issue remains the responsibility of the owner.

Leaders understand that they serve people best by acting with compassionate detachment. Human support creates a safe environment through empathy and compassion where individuals can effectively process and resolve issues. Empathic respect allows people to learn.

Business organizations often present interesting and complex challenges for leaders. Employees do carry personal agendas and issues in organizations. Treating employees, clients, and all individuals with empathy engenders much good will and makes the organization inviting to all participants. Meaningful and lasting business relationships are forged that outlast and overcome issues or problems. Understanding and good will, followed by sincere effort, will almost always resolve daily issues and build strong team connection in a supportive environment.

Please note that this is not an invitation to coddle people when they are experiencing challenges. Rather, it is an invitation to offer people authentic, empathic support when that is required. An empathic leader builds an organization that honors, integrates, and expresses the humanity of people it employs and serves.

Principle 14

Keep Impeccable Agreements

They (leaders) learned that impeccable commitments are essential for cooperative relationships, and they require a strong foundation of personal values.
—Fred Kofman
Author of *Conscious Business*

Unless commitment is made, there are only promises and hopes...but no plans.
—Peter Drucker
Global business consultant

Consider promises as a measure of our integrity and faith in ourselves.
—Stephen R. Covey
Author of *Principle-Centered Leadership*

When we honor agreements with others, we also honor agreements that we have made with ourselves. Like so many practices that honor our own life process, keeping commitments with people is also really keeping commitments with ourselves. This principle supports a very self-honoring process. This skill allows us to know that we can depend upon ourselves. And, respecting others is self-honoring.

People then trust us to adhere to agreed-upon deliverables, feedback, time lines, and project completions. They know that we are dependable and consistent because we prove it. Both internal clients and external clients expect to receive exceptional execution from our organization. The keeping of agreements sets and maintains standards for the entire company's performance.

Leaders understand that commitments cannot be compromised, thus establishing trust and respect from individuals and teams throughout the company. When leaders are impeccable with keeping agreements, it sets an example for all participants in the production process.

Keeping commitments is the backbone of management-by-objective. Impeccability in keeping agreements is also an essential skill of leadership. It constitutes authentic leadership, leadership from within. Authentic leaders uphold agreements without exception.

Principle **15**

Distinguish Context from Content

To alter the way you are being, you must engage in the phenomenon of context. Context is the human environment that determines the limitations of your actions and the scope of results your actions can produce.

—Tracy Goss
Author of *The Last Word on Power*

Integral Leadership takes into account the external universe, and the internal universe of 'self' on the mental level, the emotional level and the spiritual/ethical level.

—Ken Wilbur
Author of *The Eye of Spirit*

As we advance in wisdom, maturity, and awareness, we are able to distinguish the *context* of any event we observe or assess. Business coaches teach observing the foreground of actions and behavior, in relation to the conscious background of thoughts and beliefs.

Dr. David Hawkins, author of *Power versus Force*, offers that at higher levels of consciousness, events are seen as part of a larger context, rather than as isolated events. Utilizing broader context offers a greater palate of meaning. He encourages leaders to observe from a larger scope and richer interpretation of reality, its context. Context supersedes a point versus counterpoint approach and seeks confluence. With context we contemplates wider and deeper meaning.

When using context, people integrate a broader perspective. They no longer see and interpret isolated incidents on the surface; they understand that the incidents are a small part within a larger whole. Incidents do not hold the same meaning or power. People no longer react but respond from an expanded understanding.

In applying context we embrace and experience broader learning. Leaders can often appreciate, interpret, and integrate a synchronous effect to understand or predict the meaning of events. Then they transcend cause and effect. Using tapestry as a metaphor, leaders see the whole cloth and do not scrutinize individual threads searching for meaning.

Principle 16

Identify and Eliminate Self-Limiting Beliefs

While we may disapprove of inappropriate behavior and poor performance, we first need to communicate and help build a sense of intrinsic worth and self-esteem, totally apart from comparisons and judgment. The power to distinguish between person and performance, and to communicate (their) intrinsic worth flows naturally out of our own sense of intrinsic worth.

—Stephen R. Covey

Self-limiting beliefs are deeply held perceptions that cause or greatly influence people's behavior. Most are rooted and develop during childhood and adolescence and appear as unresolved personal-development issues in adulthood. These beliefs become part of people's being. They feel and seem automatic and function as filters through which people view themselves and the world. Such beliefs direct people even when they are not aware of them.

Mature leaders have become aware of and have successfully acceded their self-limiting beliefs. These leaders recognize when self-limiting beliefs are likely affecting other individuals and take corrective action.

Executive and life coaches often assist others as mentors, seeking greater potential in their clients.

Effective leaders separate people from certain limiting behaviors. Leaders often assist employees and clients to integrate or transcend self-limiting beliefs. Often individuals then assume greater levels of responsibility, commitment, and success.

From my study of psychology, plus personal experience, I learned that self-limiting beliefs and behaviors develop around childhood responses to frightening or painful experiences. These beliefs arise from unconscious needs for protection or safety. In adulthood, self-limiting beliefs form a perception filter that often hinders or impedes people from venturing out or responding effectively to challenge. For leaders in business, limiting beliefs represent barriers to growth and healthy risk-taking.

The best leaders are superb mentors because they ask and challenge people to transcend their current limitations. Inspired leaders engender personal transformation and development within people, and they extend growth and learning into the culture of their organizations or business relationships. Often, these leaders hire management coaches to train managers to be mentors for employees.

I encourage leaders to mentor their employees. With mentoring, individuals can stretch into a more courageous version of themselves. Leaders intrinsically know that most people hold untapped potential. Nothing works better in motivating people than supportive encouragement. Often the leaders' recognition of their workers' abilities will motivate them to accept risks, try harder, and accede to levels previously unrealized or imagined. Effective coaches achieve these results in sports all the time. Coaching also works for organizations and business relationships.

In my coaching experience, mirroring and reflecting to the clients the good that they are is the most effective tool to help them change their beliefs about themselves. Individuals typically don't see themselves as others see them. They often are unable to see their inherent goodness. Their inner critic has been active for years, and their view of themselves is often clouded by negative self-judgments, perceptions, and unhealed issues. With effective coaching, clients begin to accept and believe in their goodness. It is gratifying to witness when an individual heals and transforms within. Clients transcend their memories, self-judgments, and self-imposed limitations. They literally become the greatness that they always were.

Leaders know that mentoring and encouraging work far better than trying to fix people. Fixing implies right versus wrong, and it perpetuates self-limiting beliefs. People resent when they are made to feel "wrong." Like poor parenting, condemning, judging, and criticizing never produce the desired effect for improvement.

Leaders have a phenomenal opportunity to create a business culture in which people are afforded consideration, respect, and nurturing. Doing this will powerfully inspire superior effort. People would run to work and enjoy themselves in this caring business environment. Separate people from their self-limiting behavior, value them for their intrinsic worth, and watch people, business relationships, and organizations flourish.

Principle 17

Give Effective Feedback Without Emotional Charge

The challenge is to be a light, not a judge; to be a model, not a critic.
—Stephen R. Covey

Learning to give effective feedback is an essential element of leadership. Feedback is honest communication, which engenders intimacy, encouragement, and growth. People's performance is often a response to who they perceive themselves to be, with us, in a team relationship. Leaders encourage contribution.

Leaders are often obligated to assess and review people's performance. Effective leaders seek to provide honest appraisals while creating optimal results as they support the person in the feedback process. Leaders emphasize what works well, rather than who works well. Creating a winning formula can prove challenging for the best leader. So, honing and refining this skill is important to every leader.

Giving effective feedback involves providing information about actions or processes. Feedback is either positively reinforcing or course-corrective. If offered with respect and consideration, either type of feedback can be valuable as it provides helpful guidance. If feedback is offered in a conducive, professional environment, it can be a powerful learning tool. When done well, feedback can be a caring request to a valued individual to achieve better results and be more effective in their role. Feedback is not an attempt to fix people; its nature and message is encouragement. Effective feedback from a nurturing leader communicates "what's right" versus "who's right."

It requires courage to honestly share perceptions and experiences with people when you have no way to gauge or anticipate their responses. Positive reinforcement feedback acknowledges and emphasizes perceived strengths. Positive feedback inspires individuals to go even further. Course-corrective feedback that cites specific issues can assist individuals in recognizing and adapting limiting attitudes, beliefs, and behaviors.

Genuine feedback can help people better align with the vision and mission of the organization or business relationship. People can recognize areas where they could learn, grow, and develop their skills and enhance themselves. Leaders demonstrate that feedback is a refining process, rather than a criticizing one.

Beware when a leader begins a feedback discussion with any of these: "Look! How did you expect...?" Or "Why didn't you...?" Or "It's unacceptable that you...." With emotionally charged openings like these, the individual is automatically put on the defensive and may become deaf to any possible value from the feedback.

However, if a leader introduces feedback with, "I have some information to share with you that may be very valuable. Would you be open to discussing this?" or

"I have some feedback which might be very useful to you and assist you. Would you be open to hearing it?" the leader has invited a productive, thought-provoking, action-oriented feedback session with the individual.

Effective feedback from leaders, without an emotional charge, benefits everyone—the individual, the organization, its clients, and its stakeholders. Effective feedback builds effective organizations.

Principle 18

Confronting with Compassionate Caring

Love is always creative and fear is always destructive.
—Emmett Fox, philosopher and theologian

Amazing value is created when leaders caringly share information from their authentic center in relationships. "Care-frontation" embraces honesty. Choosing to leave issues unresolved does not serve the interests of anyone. Relationships lose their authentic bond when truth is withheld. Relationships lose trust because they are no longer experienced as authentic.

Often it takes courage to speak truthfully. However, truthfully saying what needs to be said in a respectful way is honoring the other person. The spirit of sharing honest feedback is to inform and resolve issues whenever it is possible to do so. "Care-frontation" is an invitation to influence people without harming them though confrontation.

Confrontation usually involves sudden, blind or callous indifference to another's feelings. "Care-frontation" is honoring and assists individuals in reassessing a situation. It gives them the ability to respond from within an honest, caring relationship. A relationship can greatly expand if individuals respond with integrity, truth, and mutual respect. "Care-fronting" can empower people to own their feelings, responses, and decisions.

Honest communication occurs when participants combine the head and heart. The key skill is both what is stated and how it is delivered. If leaders speak authentically from their experience and remain true to their experience, the respondent now has meaningful, useful information to make accurate, valid, and self-directed choices. Choosing "care-frontation" is not people pleasing; rather it is direct but loving.

"Care-frontation" usually is introduced with an honoring, kind opening statement, such as:

"Perhaps you are not aware of this, but I feel compelled to share something. Are you open to some coaching on an issue?" or "Maybe I didn't clearly explain my expectation, but I really need to communicate some feedback with you. Would you be willing to listen?"

The communication is solely to put things right, within the context of a caring relationship. Using a gentle approach leaves room for openness and invites people to communicate, rather than defend their words or behavior. People can authentically own their responses and consciously choose their appropriate action.

The individuals can consciously choose to weigh and balance what is important and valued within their communication and the relationship. Because people recognize and appreciate sincere concern, the individuals involved have the opportunity to construct, navigate, and honor one another. Decisions can be made within honest, authentic boundaries, and the relationship is nurtured through the difficulty.

Principle 19

Request Continuous Feedback

I not only use all the brains I have, but all the brains I can borrow.
—Woodrow Wilson, U.S. President

Effective leaders continually gather intelligence, updates, surveillance, and feedback from other leaders. They are like airline pilots who communicate with air traffic controllers and other pilots to gather information and assess the entire landscape.

Effective leaders use all available information from the cumulative power of many minds. Leaders often ask open-ended questions to gather meaningful information from others and assess the big picture. Open-ended questions could sound like this: "How are we doing?" or "Where are we in the process?" or "What can we do to improve...?" or "How could we be more efficient?"

Leaders who seek and give effective feedback set an example for people to follow. People then feel comfortable to inquire, and to give to and receive feedback from each other. They exchange ideas and make unique contributions. Feedback fosters collaboration and furthers effective communication.

In *Good to Great*, Jim Collins suggests that communicating and good business practice must extend across the entire organization. Most published authorities on leadership emphasize the importance of incremental improvement through implementation, continuous feedback, evaluation, and measurement in their writing.

For leaders, continuous feedback is a core skill that encourages creative participation, learning, and improvement throughout the entire organization. As companies adapt in the environment of continuous change, continuous feedback is the principle behind course-corrective leadership action.

Principle 20

Never Reward or Ignore Unacceptable Behavior

When we give in to irresponsible behavior by excusing it or sympathizing with it, we condone and foster spoiled, law-unto-itself behavior. And if we give in—by ignoring people or tearing into them—we undermine their motivation to try.

—Stephen R. Covey

Nurturing and concern are key components of the Never Reward or Ignore Unacceptable Behavior principle. True leaders view this as an opportunity to set an example and demonstrate compassionate boundary setting. Leaders clearly communicate behavior limits. In a calm, resolute manner, they delineate actions that are unacceptable in a business environment and cannot be tolerated. Leaders then request that people own their actions and respectfully accept accountability for their behavior. Individuals can learn and grow in constructive ways.

Leaders exercise this corrective option as course change. They will honor all employees and create and maintain a constructive, respectful business environment. If the leader's intention is to teach and improve, rather than punish, the entire organization is served. All individuals must contribute and participate in upholding relationships within the business. The leader's skill, in addressing people with genuine concern and support while requiring improvement, is the key to a successful outcome.

Leaders choose actions that set an example and meet a higher standard. Ideally, they provide caring and support, which encourages employees to act from a higher standard as well. If demonstrated by conscientious example, employees may choose to respond in kind.

Principle 21

First Understand, and Then Be Understood

Grant that I not so much seek to be understood as to understand.
—*Prayer of St. Francis of Assisi*

A majority of leadership activity involves effective communication. The goal of understanding and being understood is to honestly communicate from objective, personal experience. Leaders comprehend that understanding and being understood involves dual skills.

To **understand**, leaders must **listen effectively**.

To **be understood**, leaders must **speak effectively**.

Effective leaders listen intently to understand, and they speak succinctly to express themselves. To engender mutual understanding, the communication is sincere and respectful. Leaders communicate positively, which fosters understanding; negative emotion or speech only lowers the energy of others and distorts communication. The entire purpose of communication is to further understanding.

This skill is simple and empowering. It allows mutual self-expression and sharing in a positive setting. Remember, leaders always have the opportunity to use perception checking and to express unconditional positive regard to achieve genuine understanding.

Principle 22

Mentor, Develop, and Create New Leaders

I don't know what your destiny will be, but one thing I know, the only ones among you who will be really happy are those who have sought and found how to serve.
—Dr. Albert Schweitzer
Global humanitarian

Leaders who develop business cultures that support and nurture other leaders promulgate the growth of employees and the organization. These environments welcome and encourage high levels of self-responsibility, empowerment, assertive communication, purposefulness, and integrity. Ideally, all leaders' and employees' knowledge, expertise, and competence are valued beyond rank or title. The position people hold in an organization is no longer the key determinant of authority or value.

In *Self-Esteem at Work*, Nathaniel Branden writes that the U.S. military understands the importance of leadership training better than most organizations. Despite the contextual differences, military and business organizations share three intrinsic, transferable leadership priorities: accomplish the mission, provide and care for personnel, and create new leaders. The creation of new leaders is well understood as a vital process of leadership.

Technology has changed how all people communicate and conduct business. In today's information-centered organizations, leaders now employ knowledge workers. Knowledge workers thrive in environments where leadership development and training are cultural provisions. For information-based companies, mentoring is essential to remain current in this global network of business and communication.

On a personal level, mentoring others is very rewarding for me. In my coaching experience, clients often receive new insights and experience breakthrough moments. New energies emerge, new possibilities appear, and new choices become available to them. Without exception, clients express joy and experience expansion through personal reinvention. Whenever possible, I embrace an opportunity to develop and guide other leaders and learn from them as well.

Leaders bring out the best in people. Mentoring benefits organizations, business relationships, and communities. Creating new leaders is an exciting endeavor that serves the higher good.

Principle 23

Practice Conscious Leadership

I believe what is missing, most fundamentally, is a deep understanding of what it means to develop an organization as a conscious human community.
— Fred Kofman,
Author of *Conscious Leadership*

Embedded in culture is communication, and 90% of communication is subliminal.
—William Guillory
Author of *Spirituality in the Workplace*

In *Conscious Leadership*, Fred Kofman says: "When we are conscious, we can better perceive our surroundings, understand our situation, remember what's important to us, and envision more possibilities or action to attain it. Consciousness enables us to face our circumstances and pursue our goals in alignment with our values."

Corporate culture is often composed of accepted beliefs and chosen core values of the organizations' founders and leaders. A conscious culture mandates that those intrinsic values are in alignment with spiritual and ethical considerations. The cultural beliefs inculcate the greater good of all stakeholders.

Communication and culture are inseparable. Conscious leaders are excellent communicators who possess a formidable sense of integrity and fair play and who negotiate for "win-win" outcomes. They are often rigorously organized and hold themselves to impeccable levels of responsibility and accountability. Effective leaders author their own genuine, authentic world and demonstrate mastery in business and life pursuits.

Conscious leaders integrate an advanced intellect with emotional intelligence and ethical context to serve a higher good for all stakeholders. Fred Kofman refers to this masterful balance of leadership consciousness as ontological humility.

Kofman offers that, "Nothing is more vital for exceptional (human) performance than conscious management." Cultural alignment and cohesion are hallmarks of the conscious culture. Conscious leaders create conducive environments where people blossom and contribute as professionals and conscious individuals. Conscious culture underpins the greatest good for all stakeholders of the organization and the community.

Principle 24

Integrate Commerce
with Community

While business is a game of numbers, real achievement is measured in infinite emotional wealth: friendship, usefulness, helping, learning or, said another way, he who dies with the most joys wins!
—Dale Dauten, Syndicated Columnist,
The Corporate Curmudgeon
Author of *(Great) Employees Only* and
The Gifted Boss

An entrepreneur is an artist who is not afraid of commerce or money.
—Steve Chandler
Co-author of *100 Ways to Create Wealth*

The most important dimension of business remains unchanged. Any successful business serves the needs of a community or some population of clients. When a company gives superior service and builds meaningful bonds of caring within its community, success is inevitable. Moreover, the company becomes more than a business; the company itself becomes a community within a community.

A company that serves as a community focuses on serving the greater community from within. An organization structured in this way becomes a community of shared responsibility, mutual learning, shared experience, and delegated authority for one purpose. That purpose is to serve a community as a community.

In the hectic pace of today, leaders have an unprecedented opportunity to focus their business in a more personalized fashion. They can create the company to be a business from the same cultural values as familial, charitable or spiritual communities, whose center is caring and respect for those they serve. The same is true for small business or larger organizations because human fundamentals are universal. Clients appreciate personalized concern and sincerity.

The conscious business community supports common objectives with shared goals and *genuine* meaning for all. The care of clients becomes the central fabric of the organization. Individuals are empowered to take unprecedented responsibility for their role in changing the environment from one of "me" to one of "we." When employees accede to share responsibility, team alignment becomes the focus for creating personal and organizational service.

When leaders create companies that are communities, individuals with their unique, creative ideas and innovations become key resources in the organization. Cultural capital becomes a competitive advantage in the 21st Century business. For further reading on this contemporary approach, I recommend *Liberating the Corporate Soul* by Richard Barrett. He ingeniously expands theories of cultural refinement and enhancement. He has developed methods of value measurement to enhance business culture and practice. His own organization is built on reinventing clients' organizations through cultural refinements and systems change.

Principle 25

Focus First on Goals, Then Results

The best way to predict the future is to invent it.

—Peter Drucker

Objects of focused attention always grow. What counts is not what the goals are, but what they represent and who they serve. They are the roadmap to the success one desires. Leaders would not dream of driving to a city of unknown location without directions. Trying to pursue success without a map is also futile. That is why a goal plan is so important.

I have read many authors' views on success. What they all recommend is that we think about what we do want and avoid focusing on what we do not want. There is no better way to focus than to create a plan and then create the discipline (actions) in carrying it out.

Over the past several years, I have learned much about how the mind controls the brain. The brain will produce the behavior that it is programmed to perform. One author calls it an "invented future." I have also heard the brain referred to as a "biocomputer," and it is just that.

When individuals or leaders shift the mind to goal orientation, success becomes a rational process. When goals are completed, the results become inevitable. Results and success go hand in hand because results are what is rewarded in business.

That is why the process starts with focused intention and motivated goal setting. When leaders teach individuals to set realistic goals *in writing*, the individuals start to program the biocomputer. They think about those goals and create a plan for how to achieve them. When the plan is completed, all that's necessary is a disciplined routine to work the plan. With each action step, one is closer to meeting the desired goals. It is a logical process. That is why goals work and motivated leaders insist on them, so the people will think about those goals continually.

Leaders know you *are* worthy of success so your goals, your plan, and your disciplined routine will reward you with the fruits of your efforts. There's nothing more rewarding than results because success is its own reward.

Principle 26

Be a Catalyst for Change

Every organization must be prepared to abandon everything it does to survive in the future.

—Peter Drucker

If change opens new doors to human betterment, it is viewed positively as a source of new opportunities. Without change, there would be no growth or development, no creative breakthroughs or discoveries, no becoming. Change brings with it its own kind of organization, like a river flowing, and we do not seem to be learning that.

—Frederic M Hudson
Author of *The Adult Years*

Effective leaders acknowledge and embrace change and manage toward it. They study where and how the environment may adapt and promulgate change within the organization. They welcome change and accelerate their organization's progression. They move out in front of the anticipated change in leading and directing.

At an M.I.T. leadership forum I attended some years ago, real estate developer Hank Spaulding surprised members of his seminar audience when he stated emphatically: *"If you don't manage your business as if it's already in trouble, it soon will be."* I have never forgotten these words. They advise leaders to remain vigilant in knowing competitive standing, market position, new product launches, new service deliveries, technology changes, and changes in consumer preferences and demand.

My first coach, Hal Rose, often stated, "If it's not broken, break it." He advised people not to become complacent. He urged leaders to constantly redefine the business environment and adapt their internal business practices. He knew intuitively that most people dread change. He also understood that the only way to overcome fear of change was to make change a norm or constant in the organization. In essence, "Change or be changed."

Stephen Chandler has written, "Confident leaders do not apologize for change." Leaders who resist change engender the potential for discouragement and low morale in employees. Change is inevitable. Change literally makes possible creating new things in new ways with new energy. It awakens us from the monotony of "sameness." Embracing change incorporates risk taking as well.

How change is perceived is very important. Effective leaders serve as catalysts and advocates for change. Leaders should endorse an organization that is constantly adapting, refining, and re-inventing itself to higher levels of innovation and productivity. Leaders envision and guide their organization to optimal positioning and performance.

When change is made intentionally and proactively, the change is positive and highly motivational. Hands-on leaders lean toward the upside, assess risks, and guide the organization forward. Leaders communicate the upside that reconnects people to the mission and values of the organization.

Leaders who embrace intentional change recognize adaptability as an ideal mode of operation for dynamic, conscious organizations.

Principle 27

Lead by Doing

In visionary companies, the drive for progress arises from a deep human urge— to explore, to create, to change, to improve. It's a deep inner, compulsive—almost primal—drive.
—James C. Collins and Jerry I. Porrus
Authors of *Built to Last*

Leading by doing works as a most durable, long-lasting motivational skill. Especially in small or medium-sized businesses, effective leaders only ask employees to perform tasks that they themselves would be willing to perform. Doing is the genesis of a participatory leadership style and setting.

Leading by doing embodies the essence of true teamwork. Taking action raises self-esteem and energy levels for the leaders and the team. Teamwork builds synchronicity and fun. Although leaders may be acknowledged as the owners of teams and projects, leaders are also integral team members. They co-create desired results as functional team members.

This skill bonds leaders with employees and effectively removes any "us versus them" perceptions. This leadership approach serves as a powerful antidote to controlling, to hierarchical "leadership" and management structure. Leading by doing neutralizes any perceived effects of manipulation or of patriarchal power structures.

Effective leaders function as dutiful supporters and functional team players. Effective leaders are active participants, not "chief" spectators.

Principle 28

Recruit and Hire Motivated Talent

In the great mass of our people, there are plenty individuals of intelligence from among whom leadership can be recruited.
—Herbert Hoover

I hire people brighter than me, and then I get out of their way.
—Lee Iacocca

Interviewing is an art form. Leaders give effective interviews when they really get to know people. It is well known that many candidates have the skills and experience to perform the job. However, leaders whose organizations endorse finding "fit" need to gauge people beyond their presentation.

Effective interviewers ask open-ended questions. This artful approach puts candidates at ease and offers them an opportunity to express and share more of themselves. People enjoy discussing the things that interest and inspire them.

Leaders may encourage people to discuss their hobbies and interests. If individuals are interested and involved in community service, they generally enjoy providing selfless service that may be an indicator of their essence, demeanor, and nature with other people. This is the art of the interview.

After posing initial questions, leaders often ask people, "Can you tell me more about that?" or "I'd like to hear more." or "Would you please elaborate on that?" This method of inquiring is called *layering*. The interviewers, through this process, receive a miniature life story; they know more of the candidate's professional attributes, personal pursuits, and internal values.

Leaders then move into the science part of interviews. They inquire about people's motivations and interest in the organization. If individuals limit their responses to income or job description, they indicate that they may not be an optimal choice for hiring.

If candidates research the mission and the organization's background or say that the mission or culture is appealing, a new conversation may develop. Leaders seek people with motivation, experience, responsibility, and willingness who contribute to their team to advance the organization's vision and mission.

Principle 29

Reinvent, Renew, and Refine Consciously

Reinvention =>   Process/Systems
Renewal =>   People
Refinement =>   Culture/Beliefs/Values

I chose to diagram and divide this principle into equal parts to illustrate that people, systems, and beliefs are inextricably related yet retain distinct elements that differentiate them. Systems and processes are inanimate. People are living, dynamic beings. Culture, beliefs, and values are real, both subliminal and dynamic.

Reinvention is the process of continuous, incremental improvement of processes and systems. I call it the internal drive within organizations. Leaders use efficiency models to reallocate resources to increase productivity. Effective systems and processes allow leaders to drive change so that organizations thrive as evolving enterprises. When applied well, these systems and processes create a vibrant, growing, and stable organization.

Renewal is a form of refurbishment and refueling for people. Jim Loehr and Tony Schwartz discuss renewal in *The Power of Full Engagement*. Renewal involves the human being balancing the physical, mental, emotional, and spiritual levels. An effective individual is one who is congruent with all four of these levels in life. Leaders provide an environment where people can be fully engaged with periodic renewal.

Refinement is derived from revisiting the vision and mission. It requires that people ask themselves, "Whom do we serve? ... What gives this important work meaning? ... How do we derive fulfillment from performing this work with excellence? How can we be impeccable as an organization?" People's responses act as beacons to clients, communities, industries, and the world.

Together these three processes constitute renewal from within. Leaders who utilize and support these three processes create organizations that can adapt, improve, and expand with a natural flow of self-regenerating resources.

Principle 30

Foster Self-Confidence and Self-Esteem

Outstanding leaders go out of their way to boost the self-esteem of their personnel. If people believe in themselves, it's amazing what they can accomplish.

—Sam Walton
Founder of Wal-Mart

Leaders have a powerful influence over how their people are viewed and greatly influence their potential. In *Principle-Centered Leadership*, Stephen Covey emphasizes that leaders preserve and support positive self-esteem through giving their people feedback and positive regard. He writes, "While we may disapprove of inappropriate behavior and poor performance, we first need to communicate and help build a sense of (their) intrinsic worth and self-esteem *totally apart from comparisons and judgments*. The result will inspire superior effort."

Great leaders express genuine concern for their people. Esteem becomes part of the culture. Leaders create a new possibility for those around them, and communicate this new possibility as who they are, guided by the leader. The dynamic where they believe this possibility from the leader is based in esteem.

Nothing builds self-esteem like success. Success is often the result of the perception that leaders reward. Steve Chandler writes, "You get what you reward."

When leaders reward success, people's levels of confidence soar.

As they receive rewards, employees feel esteemed because they attract and achieve success. Success and achievement are magnetic in nature; they become contagious in organizations. Leaders who reinforce success automatically create motivated and confident individuals. Success is its own reward because team confidence and employee self-esteem soar.

Leaders benefit from success and value their people's collective efforts. Positive affirmation rewards collective success, and a win/win situation exists for leaders and employees. In leadership environments that welcome and reward success, people not only succeed but also satisfy their need for individual and collective meaning in the company culture.

Principle 31

Engender a Culture of Trust

Great managers, i.e., great leaders, earn the trust and respect of their 'subordinates.' Without trust and respect, followers will rarely exert more than a minimal effort in the pursuit of the goals set by a leader.

—Fred Kofman

Building a trust culture is the "spine" of any successful business culture. No one sets the tone and affects the mood of an organization more than its leaders. Leaders must lead by doing to inspire employees. Mutual trust emerges from leaders who function as centers of authentic power. Effective leaders foster cultures of mutual trust when they welcome and encourage people to bring their true conscious selves to work to create, take risks, and innovate. People, products, services, and processes improve and thrive in this conducive business environment.

The culture of trust becomes the foundation of an ongoing process of self-expression, organizational improvement, and refinement. Employees are encouraged to express ideas in an open forum, where choices are parsed and possibilities vetted as items under consideration for leadership-endorsed strategy. The team openly and candidly debates tactical issues using the collective power of many minds. Employees receive buy-in, and best business practices become the collective goal and everyday process.

When trust exists, sharing of information flows across the organization. Individuals accept responsibility and empowerment to innovate. Furthermore, when trust is inherent within the organization, creativity of all individuals is encouraged and expected. With trust, the entire organization participates in creating optimal business practices for the greatest good of all stakeholders. Through a culture of trust, the leaders can build organizations where information and communication flow freely where people want to work and share their valued resources openly.

Principle **32**

Use Enthusiasm To Inspire Vision

Nothing great was ever created without enthusiasm.

—Ralph Waldo Emerson

The word **inspiration** comes from the Latin root *in spirito*, which means of spirit. The word *enthusiasm* comes from the Greek root *en theos*, which means from God. These early, advanced cultures intuited that higher guidance played a significant role in creating their societies' advanced vision.

Leaders create powerful visions and serve as emissaries and advocates who welcome people to share their vision. The leader's passion creates the vision, and that passion translates into enthusiasm for others. How could leaders who create great organizations not be excited and enthusiastic?

To coin a popular phrase, this is where the rubber meets the road. People in management often inherit a position in an organization and hold a biased belief that the function must be preserved, as it is. There is no vision or inspiration in that approach. There is little ownership or enthusiasm if individuals cannot create and expand their respective roles. Without enthusiastic ownership there is no opportunity and there will be no new vision.

Leading with enthusiasm and inspiration generates internal excitement that actually advances organizations. Their vision and mission statements move from vague philosophies as static documents to living, dynamic creative processes. Organizations' strategies become credos that inspire people to produce superior services and products. When enthusiasm is present, individuals have incentive to think deeply. All great ideas come from inspired thinking.

Enthusiasm is magnetic and contagious. Employees enjoy joining organizations that design and create excellence from great excitement. They derive satisfaction and pride from work. Their need for collective meaning is fulfilling. In such an organization, success itself becomes a generator of enthusiasm.

A leader with a compelling vision has an abundant opportunity to spread that passion. Enthusiastic leadership encourages people to share the vision, embrace enthusiasm, and propel the vision forward.

Principle 33

See the Upside

The reason that pessimism is the most fundamental mistake that leaders can make is that we are always surrounded with the "downside" of any decisions and variables.

—Steve Chandler

Leaders always look for the upside and move toward success. They understand that the very future of their organizations hinges on their outlook. Effective leaders consider and mitigate the downside but always maintain a positive focus. Leaders relentlessly focus upon the upside.

It is a warped viewpoint to examine the downside without looking for the upside. Leaders certainly exhibit fortitude and assume risk when they choose to see the upside. No winning strategy is without risk, and with risk comes reward.

Steve Chandler speaks to genuine leadership when he writes:

Optimistic leaders acknowledge the downside of every situation, then focus on the majority of their thinking on the upside. They also focus the majority of the communication on the upside. They know the downside is always well known throughout the team. But the upside is never as well known. Who wants to look like an idiotic optimist? It is far more popular and easy to be a clever and witty pessimist. But it is not leadership.

Steadfast leaders intuitively know that vision, potential, and new possibilities are generated by seeing the upside.

Principle 34

Recognize, Reinforce, and Reward as Motivation

The deepest principle in human nature is the craving to be appreciated.
—William James, (1842-1910)
Pioneering psychologist & philosopher

Effective leaders appreciate that motivation is positive reinforcement of desired results. Positive recognition is the most effective incentive for reaching achievement. Upbeat motivation has a much greater impact and is longer lasting than any other form of seeking results. Individuals feel invited to be successful. Leaders who choose rewarding and authentic recognition forge powerful, lasting bonds with people.

Leaders who reward good performance receive good performance. Poor leaders tend to practice amateur therapy by attempting to fix employees or function as firefighters. Using the forest and trees analogy, ineffective leaders spend considerable time, energy, and effort on immediate issues and only see one tree. Effective leaders focus their attention and efforts on rewarding all people. They acknowledge that they may lose one tree but save the forest.

Skilled leaders spend time motivating by rewarding everyday. Rewarding is such powerful encouragement. Leaders motivate and encourage when they recognize an individual's effort through a note, an e-mail, or a phone call. That "job well done" affirmation speaks volumes, and its positive effects will last days or weeks. On the other hand, negative criticism will last months and may never be forgotten. These smaller personal gestures are meaningful and often have equal or greater effect as public recognition, prizes, bonuses, and financial incentives.

Rewarding is a special type of gratitude. Motivation and reward increase team productivity and individual effort. The game of competing makes competition more enjoyable because people are competing for the fun and the reward. It makes winning a psychological challenge.

Leaders who wisely invest time and effort rewarding employees create highly motivational environments where individuals feel genuine incentives to generate great results.

Principle 35

Master Thoughts and Emotions

What we are today comes from our thoughts of yesterday, and our present thoughts build our lives of tomorrow. Our life is the creation of the mind.
—Siddhartha Gautama, the Buddha

Great men are they who see that thought is stronger than any material force, that thought rules the world.
—Ralph Waldo Emerson

Leadership involves being very selective about our thinking. One of the greatest insights I ever learned is that every emotion I experience is an effect of my own thinking. Great gifts often come with great responsibility. I am responsible for what I think and feel, no one else. Eleanor Roosevelt used to joke that no one could provoke her without her permission.

Dr. David D. Burns' book, *Feeling Good*, has some very powerful insights into the realm of thoughts and emotions. Dr. Burns explains that people's feelings don't spawn their thoughts. The reverse is true; thoughts stimulate feelings and can generate or prolong people's moods. I became so fascinated with the inner workings of the mind that I decided to pursue graduate study in spiritual psychology at the University of Santa Monica.

As thoughts are powerful programming, individuals need to be diligently conscious of what they think and where their thoughts dwell. People literally manifest into their lives what they expect. People's thinking determines their perspective and molds their entire existence.

There is a wisdom parable about two medieval men that demonstrates the power of thought and perspective. Both men are stonecutters, performing the same task to construct buildings. The first man thinks, "I am continually, repeatedly cutting this dreary, cold stone." The second man thinks, "I am building a great cathedral to the Divine which will be glorious and last for all time." Thought can generate such different perspective and yield very different energy levels and results.

Monitoring feelings is also an important skill. Emotions are companions to thoughts and beliefs. Applied psychologists often describe emotions as "E-motion" or energy-in-motion. As leaders learn to master their thought, they also discover how to monitor emotions and harness their energy. Mastery over thoughts and emotions, while preserving valuable energy, is an advanced leadership skill.

In my Mastermind group, I recently discovered another superb book on the effects our thinking produces in our personal lives. In *The Relationship Handbook*, by George Pransky, there are many wonderful insights into the impact our thinking and moods can project into our interactions with others. I recommend it to any leader who intends to seek greater dominion over thoughts and feelings and to enjoy rewarding personal and professional relationships.

Advanced leaders master their thoughts and integrate their emotions to create successful results for themselves and the people they lead. They achieve mastery over mind to manifest solid relationships and generate optimal outcomes.

Principle 36

Assume Full Responsibility

Owners invent the situation; victims blame the situation.

—Steve Chandler

If you think you can't, then you won't.

—Dwight D. Eisenhower

When Steve Chandler leads group trainings, he often states, "Victims blame, whereas owners create." The reason Steve is such an effective motivational trainer is that he assists people to recognize where they feel stuck or are unable to take action. They are often engaging in lower thinking from ego, rather than higher thinking of creation.

Victims and owners listen to different internal mental scripts and carry distinctly different energies.

Victims espouse, "Life manipulates me, controls me, and does _____ to me; I am a victim of circumstance." Life is seen as a trap or a dead end.

The internal victim script translates into: "I will never get anywhere. I am not good enough. Other people have all the luck. I will have to tolerate and put up with what comes my way. I will plod along, muddle through, and get by."

The energy of the victim stance equals: *I survive and get by. Life is hopeless.*

Owners believe, "I use life to produce and have _____. I am capable, creative, and fully empowered to make a good life for myself and others. I am on a mission to achieve and succeed." Life is seen as an opportunity to create.

The internal owner script translates into: "I will make my own successful world within the greater universe. I am capable of achieving what I desire and choose for myself and others. Life is a wonder-filled adventure and a challenge where I can learn to create and manifest my dreams."

The energy of the owner stance equals: *I thrive and I'm in charge.*

Fred Kofman and Stephen Covey discuss victim versus owner concepts for leaders in their books. These authors suggest that leaders request that their people assume full responsibility to rise above their negative inner script. Leaders ask employees to move beyond "I can't" or "I am a victim of circumstances" responses and approaches to problem solving.

Inspired leaders have a phenomenal opportunity to encourage individuals to take full responsibility. Overcoming limitation and self-victimizing patterns can liberate individuals into lives of contribution and meaning. Leaders who provide the atmosphere of self-empowerment can literally shift the organization one person at a time.

Principle 37

Create Using Intention and Focused Action

> *You become what you think. You receive what you focus upon.*
> —Norman Vincent Peale,
> *The Power of Positive Thinking*

Many brilliant authors of the last century have written about creation using the mind. Napolean Hill, Ernest Holmes, and Emmett Fox introduced the concept that people are all gifted, creative beings full of potential. People are capable of creating great things with this inner potential. When people choose pursuits to serve others toward the highest good, they become conscious creators. Their potential expands as it aligns with good.

When people consciously create toward higher pursuits, they activate a source of universal assistance. This source is potential realized within them. It is unlimited, available, and accessible to them at all times. Once people "set their mind to something" with clear, positive intention, the source mind assists them from within. Carl Jung called this phenomenon or source *synchronicity.* As individuals experience synchronicity, they know they are on the right track.

Conscious leaders create organizations and business relationships that recognize and encourage synchronistic potential in people. They set clear intentions, focus on objectives with clarity, and develop action plans that are carried out in pursuit of those desired goals.

Leaders focus on achieving effective results rather than mere attempts or methods. I have personally stopped using the word "try." "Try" implies that one is already receiving an *out* when they say "I'll try." Instead, I suggest that you choose to say, "I will..." or "I commit to..." Those are terms of action; they commit to action.

My first coach, Hal Rose, asked me to set goals of what I chose to create with clear intention. He then had me make a contract with myself in writing (which is very important) *that we both signed.* I admit to thinking this was a little "out there," but he then proceeded to explain how individuals create by activating something deep within themselves.

He taught me the unseen power of setting clear intentions consciously and making and keeping commitments to myself by taking action. This is far more than "going through the motions" or making a to-do list and checking off items as you complete tasks. It is conscious thought followed by focused action.

Hal directed me to make contracts with myself and fulfill them without fail. He also explained that if I do not keep and fulfill these agreements with myself, I would be limiting my potential to think, act, and attract. By asking me to sign those contracts with myself, he was showing me the difference between a thought and an idea, a dream versus a vision, and the relationship between actions and beliefs.

I realized that positive thinking only scratched the surface. Positive thinking must be followed by committed action to create results. Without the deep *intention* or belief and fully engaged *commitment* or action, my goals remain only at the level of thought.

When people's intention becomes deeply held conviction and they take action, energy is created and released. Dr. David Hawkins, author of *Power Versus*

Force, explains in his lectures that this energy phenomenon actually operates on the quantum level. To paraphrase, a person's intention is met by potential—the Quantum energy field—to manifest actuality or reality in the physical realm. This is a quantum understanding of realizing potential, co-creating, and manifesting reality from intention.

Leaders who commit deeply to intention and execution through their people, foster potential in others. Leaders can provide exemplary demonstration of following good planning by effective action. Leadership vision manifests into reality, one action step at a time.

Principle 38

Design Teams with Multiple Leaders

... Leadership transforms individual potential into collective performance...
—Fred Kofman

Leaders can't go it alone. The outdated view that businesses leaders as sole brilliant visionaries who had to think, create, and develop everything is shortsighted.

More resources are better than few. Combining the multiple talents of leader teams creates synergy and momentum. A collective mind trust of a talented leadership team comprises a new, conscious business model for 21st Century organizations.

In their book, *The Power of Full Engagement*, Loehr and Schwartz promulgate great business practices. They suggest that wisdom for leaders lies in the *ability to manage their precious energy*. Committed leaders direct energy toward maximally productive endeavors that flow. With a team of leaders, delegation to other leaders with varying expertise leverages energy. They propel action with focus and energy, assisted by teams.

Loehr and Schwartz imply that no leader or individual person is exceptional at everything so leaders need to know where people excel. Leaders utilize delegation and shared responsibility to create effective teams of leaders for larger organizations.

Conscious leaders create teams of leaders who work

as participating servants within the organization. With a participatory management practice, talent, skill, and creative ideas grow exponentially in these leadership teams. Their results propel organizations beyond the current upper limits.

Principle 39

Manage Relationships with Clear Agreements

Management is focused on projects. A manager manages agreements that lead to successful completion of those projects. Managing agreements elevates the person that you're managing and leading to a much more professional level. When you manage agreements, you're partnering together as co-professionals with a common goal. That's the best kind of leadership. You manage a project and you manage input, throughput, and output, but you don't manage people. You lead people by managing agreements.

—Duane Black and Steve Chandler
Authors of *The Hands Off Manager*

Most of us recognize that we cannot change others, so why do we believe that we can manage others? Leaders cannot manage other people's emotions and personalities, but they can influence their goals and priorities through responsible agreements. Leaders manage their agreements to have others honor what they have deemed important and then seek buy-in from them.

Leaders who believe that they can manage other people are spending their time putting out fires. These firefighters react, rather than guide their teams. Only their leftover or residual energy then goes to assist teams, almost as an afterthought. In this scenario, leading becomes a lower-tier priority and activity. Managing relationships places leadership as an upper-tier priority.

Besides fighting fires, another ineffective activity is when leaders spend the majority of their time mentoring low-end performers. The irony is that many low-end performers don't invest in their work and simply exist. As a result, precious energy, time, and mentoring resources are <u>not</u> given to mid- and top-level performers.

Leaders who expend excessive energy on low-end performers are inadvertently rewarding dysfunctional behavior and holding back organizations. Often leaders aspire that the low-end performers will advance with assistance. Research indicates that this rarely happens.

To this point, Scott Richardson and Steve Chandler have written: "This leads to poor time management and a lot of ineffective, amateur psychotherapy. It also encourages employees to take a more immature position in their communication with management, almost an attempt to be re-parented by a supervisor rather than having an adult-to-adult relationship."

Each time a leader manages with a clear agreement, he has created a team of mutual responsibility. This is a powerful application of management by objective. When individuals accept priorities by executing clear agreements, all organizational objectives are advanced. The most effective paradigm of leadership is self-management, when each individual accepts and fulfills clear agreements.

Principle **40**

Provide Extraordinary Value

The vast majority of companies never become great, precisely because the vast majority become quite good—and that is their main problem.

—Jim Collins
Author of *Good to Great*

Extraordinary value is defined as giving clients or customers three to ten times the amount of value as your fee would dictate. Leaders who embrace this practice enjoy a superb competitive advantage. They know that if their organizations provide this exceptional value to clients, they will have few real competitors.

The spirit of service is the ability to make a contribution. The greater the contribution, the greater the value received. Companies that deliver extraordinary client service care about clients' businesses as much as they do. As clients receive extraordinary value, they become continual sources of referrals. Person- to-person referrals are often believed to be the most effective form of new business creation.

Extraordinary value creation is not found in the pure quantity of the product/ service rendered, but rather in the underlying spirit of the intention and energy of the provider. In my coaching practice, one client wrote a testimonial stating that I didn't offer canned, cookie-cutter solutions. I facilitated a process that allowed him to look deep within, to experience new aspects, and to feel empowered and capable of handling anything. The client learned that the answer had already been within him to now experience and express self-trust, self-esteem, and self-confidence. When clients receive guidance from their own internal compass, discovery of a whole new level results. They are empowered to discern what processes best support them, not only in the present, but also for a lifetime. To borrow from the MasterCard advertisement: Priceless!

It only takes good intention and thoughtfulness to provide extraordinary value in any business. Leaders in business of any type or size from a physician to a plumber to an automobile mechanic may participate in this extraordinary value- creation process. For a physician, giving the clients adequate time and heart-centered concern for their health challenge would be light years ahead of the managed care "rush them through" model. For a plumber, it could mean having a clean, tidy uniformed crew instead of the typical crew with greasy overalls and grimy hands working in a client's beautiful home. For an automobile mechanic, it could be creating a level of trust where clients are sold only services and repairs that are needed and not overcharged. Then the auto is returned in a timely fashion.

Conscious leaders fully understand that "extraordinary value" creation is centered in intention toward the higher good for all. Clearly, when exceptional value exceeds the fee, the leader has created an extraordinary business. The leader has ensured that the clients feel served, valued, and appreciated.

Principle 41

Create a Thoughtful Brand

Any imagery which is external to the product or service and which elicits emotional feelings and identification with the product is brand.

—Kirk Souder,
Creative marketing and brand consultant

Kirk Souder has founded two remarkable companies and is a successful creative advertising and marketing executive. He has an ingenious penchant for branding. He once shared with me, "Do you want to be *Something for Everyone* or *Everything to Someone*?" These are powerful ideas and questions to consider.

Creative leaders strive to share a powerful product and service message that garners client engagement, identification, and psychological acceptance. Brand can be thought of as the "humanity" surrounding the product or service. In conscious companies, the brand messages communicate the values and mission of the leaders and company.

Leaders ask themselves, "To *whom* does the product or service appeal?" (target market segment/demand) and "*Why* does the product or service appeal to them?" (emotional appeal/brand identity).

Entertainment and media leaders create brands called treatments to make their productions appealing. They meticulously research their target audiences and refine their treatments to enhance their audience, box office, Internet, and syndication appeal. These producer leaders grasp how discerning audiences are when spending entertainment dollars, so they painstakingly weigh these marketing variables and tendencies.

Effective brands capture the imagination. Leaders also have the ability to emulate their established values and product integrity in creating responsible brand. Generating emotional appeal and brand identity for clients in their intended markets is functional. Capturing alluring concepts and packaging the spirit of the company is sublime.

Principle 42

Develop Leaders as Stewards to One Global Community

We cannot separate the healing of the individual from the healing of the planet. They are one and the same, because the consciousness of each individual is connected to the collective consciousness. Although we are individuals, we are also each part of the whole.

—Shakti Gawain
Author of *Creative Visualization*

... This challenge requires a global consciousness, a reverence for the one environment shared by all, the presence of new forms of capitalistic cooperativeness, new solutions to glaring economic inequities, and experimentation with international teams and alliances.

—Frederic M. Hudson
Author of *The Adult Years*

The love of awakened motherhood is a loving compassion, not only for one's own children but for all people, animals, plants, rocks, and rivers. It is a love extended to all nature's beings...every creature is her child.

—Ammachi
Known as the "hugging saint," Kerala, India

In Principle 75, I have excerpted the Seven Levels of Leadership Consciousness from *Liberating the Corporate Soul,* by Richard Barrett. The uppermost three levels of leadership actively support inclusion of the greater community and the global environment as a principle of conscious leadership. While these three levels may be construed as "advanced" or "evolved" leadership, it is never too early for leaders to demonstrate their reverence for all living creatures.

As human consciousness awakens on a global scale, eco-awareness must become a leadership imperative. Spiritual and ethical considerations are a responsibility of leadership. Conscious leaders will develop and institute processes that produce services and products that are humane to all living things. Trees in rain forests and other ecosystems will regenerate. Alternate energy sources will be refined that reduce pollution and chemical emissions. Food will be grown and treated with products that replenish the earth.

Leaders must embrace that we *are* one community within a global village. This is not just an idea or concept; rather it is a universal law. *Creation,* physically and spiritually, is entrusted to all people; we are its stewards. Individuals truly don't own the planet; we are its loving tenants. Certainly we harm only ourselves when we ignore or harm living creatures and our planet home.

Two years ago, I participated in *A Course in Miracles* conference whose keynote speaker was Marianne Williamson. She spoke reverently about becoming a mother for the first time. Her articulation of the divine feminine aspect was riveting and real. She stated that mothers had saved the planet before, and her central purpose was devotion to her child and the children of the world.

Marianne Williamson also stated that she was traveling to Washington, D.C., to assist in the writing of enabling legislation, for a new U.S. Cabinet position, for a "Department of Peace" to balance the U.S. Department of Defense. I was awed and inspired by her resolutely powerful yet feminine presence and maternal global concern.

With great certainty, she stated that we may have only five to ten years to reverse the damage of depleting the rainforests, burning fossil fuels, expanding the hole in the ozone layer, and poisoning the seas with chemical waste. When I recently heard that pregnant mothers could no longer consume tuna fish due to high mercury levels, I was shocked and disappointed. I asked myself if the inmates are running the asylum. New conscious leaders are needed.

Al Gore and others have courageously clarified that mankind is affecting the balance of ecosystems and disturbing nature. It is hoped that species and systems will not be brought to extinction if eco-friendly reforms are implemented soon. I respectfully entreat and challenge leaders to become conscious of our precious planet, its abundant resources, its beautiful flora, and its lovely animal species. All are part of the one global community.

Native American tribes always embraced the earth as a dominion: we are visitors; we are stewards of the land. The planet is a gift for people to use, respect, and appreciate. All the beauty, the plants, and the animals can thrive and co-exist if conscious leaders become stewards of one global community.

Principle 43

Reinvent Work as a Vocation

Discovering our calling means living our values. It means putting our values to work by resolving to make what we do reflect who we really are. A growing number of people are expecting their work to provide daily meaning and daily bread. They want work that integrates their unique gifts and talents with the practical realities of surviving and making a living.

—Richard J. Leider
Author of *The Power of Purpose*

You will recognize your own path when you come upon it because you will suddenly have all the energy and invention you will ever need.

—Jerry Gillies
Author of *Moneylove*

We make a living by what we receive, but we make a life by what we give.

—Winston Churchill

In *The Reinvention of Work*, Matthew Fox suggests that the search for deep inner meaning is often found in work that is a higher or inspired vocation. Fox writes:

In our time, we workers are being called to reexamine our work; how we do it, whom it is helping or hurting; what it is we do; and what we might be doing if we were to let go of our present work and follow a deeper call.

This vocational work literally feeds people's souls when called to follow their passion. We answer the calling to move from work-life to life-work. Ideally leaders identify and practice their vocation in their work of creating business communities.

In his book, *The Prosperity Paradigm*, Steve D'Annunzio describes that each of us has a chosen path and a sole or soul purpose that is expressed through our work. As people perform soul-based work, they receive abundance in many forms: income, loving relationships, and recognition and rewards. They create wealth beyond money. Soul work replenishes the energy we expend because it kindles the fire in our being. We experience being "on fire" with zeal, enthusiasm, and inspired creativity. Conscious leaders welcome such inspired people to serve and produce in their thriving organizations.

Steve D'Annunzio invites leaders and all people to view careers with new eyes. Instead of identifying ourselves with possessions and acquisitions or a Have, Be, Do approach and thought system, he asks people to identify their vocation to find work that they love to do. As people find their calling or vocation work, they discover that vocation work offers them much beyond mere money and acquiring more things. They adopt a Be, Do, Have approach to work. People then experience the relationship between what Matthew Fox calls *good work* and happiness.

Awakened leaders are creating conscious business communities that welcome and encourage people's vocation work. Modern business leaders recognize the fervor of individuals who are bringing heart energy and soul purpose to the workplace. Every stakeholder of such businesses is served well by the alignment of vocation and soul purpose.

Principle 44

Unlock Right-Versus-Wrong Thinking

As positionality ceases, one becomes aware that it was the source of all prior miseries, fears, and unhappiness and that every positionality is inherently in error.
—David R. Hawkins, M.D.
Author of *Power vs. Force* and
Truth vs. Falsehood

Leaders know how to overcome situations where people hold opposing positions and feel stuck. Whether in negotiations or debating business practices, leaders successfully move through impasses by using understanding, seeking consensus, and looking for the truth between and among positions.

Taking positions is so much a part of our societal, cultural, and childhood conditioning. People have trouble identifying this in themselves because the right-versus-wrong approach is deeply imbedded in their thinking and world view. Right versus wrong is taught in schools, fostered in religious organizations, and built into government. It follows that this thinking extends into business. Leaders do not have to create business communities that adopt this approach.

Certainly people need standards and values to govern society. Law enforcement is one example. It is not the need for structure and boundaries that is in question; rather it is the application and use of the right-versus-wrong model. This model is binary. People must be on one side or the other; they never join or meet. This approach or model fosters no position other than for or against. Leaders appreciate that authentic living and working require more than limited choices. Right versus wrong only affords people two options, and that approach does not foster learning and growth. Positions become exacerbated when extreme emotion becomes involved. Right versus wrong is the source of all human conflict.

Leaders cannot allow or encourage right-versus-wrong thinking because it alienates people from each other. This approach does not foster or encourage effective teamwork, creative participation, and free expression of ideas. Business communities must create options and choices for people, processes, services, and products.

Consider how quarrels between family, friends, and colleagues often become toxic. When an individual takes the position of being right, someone else needs to be wrong. People become ensnared or stuck in a black and white dichotomy. They put a great deal of intensity and emotional charge into a position that puts distance between the people.

A far more effective approach is to consider that people's positions or approaches are merely perceptions and opinions. Everyone is entitled to their perspective and opinion, because they spring from mind. However, others need not agree with those perceptions or opinions, but they may remain respectful. Leaders foster understanding by listening and honoring people's rights to have distinct viewpoints. When hostility exists, assuaging and mitigating negative emotion is imperative.

This is an *unlocking* skill because both participants show willingness to unlock their positions while they mitigate the separation of right versus wrong. In my business experience, I have witnessed how great injury and harm can be projected onto coworkers when positionality is rampant in organizations. Judgment, blame, and condemnation based upon positions are destructive and they destroy relationships.

At my graduation from the University of Santa Monica, Dr. Ron Hulnick offered: "Peaceful relations will only become possible when individuals come to realize and begin the cessation of against-ness." I encourage leaders to think carefully about the healing power of this skill. The ultimate "positionality" on a mass level is war. It is the right-versus-wrong model expressed on a regional or global level.

Conciliatory leaders can choose beyond right-versus-wrong processes, unlock positionality, and reduce the destruction this limiting concept wreaks on all business relationships.

Principle 45

Seize the Day

Nothing is as fatiguing as the eternal hanging on of an unaccomplished task.
—William James (1842-1910)
Pioneering psychologist and philosopher

Cherish each hour of this day for it can never return.

—Og Mandino
Author of
The Greatest Salesman in the World

Roman leaders coined the phrase, *Carpe diem*, which translates to *seize the day*. Skilled leaders know the necessity of proactivity. They understand and appreciate that every moment in each day holds opportunities. Individuals with clear mind, who focus on the present moment, can envision, create, serve, and produce with grace and skill.

An old Buddhist proverb states that each day is a miniature version of your entire life. Each day will hold opportunities, gains, obstacles, and perhaps frustrations. People's perspective determines how they view these events. Individuals determine how they may use their time, energy, and focus.

Within each day, leaders have learned to manage their energy and resources effectively to best serve their company and clients. They devote their full attention and creativity to the project or priority at hand. Leaders participate and fully engage all people to functionally serve at optimal levels each day.

Principle 46

Never Accept Defeat

Never talk defeat. Use words like hope, belief, faith, and victory.
—Brendan Kennelly, Irish poet

Only you can deprive yourself of anything. Do not oppose this realization for it is truly the beginning of the dawn of light.
—*A Course in Miracles*

Patience and perseverance have a magical effect before which difficulties disappear and obstacles vanish.
—Dwight D. Eisenhower

Many people give up just short of reaching their goal, right before they have achieved the reward for their efforts. This is a subtle form of self-sabotage.

If people truly commit to goals they have set, then giving up is wasting energy. Neurological pathways and patterns are formed in our brain through the repetition of words, thoughts, and processes. The energy flow of positive intention and focus of the mind is what creates the result. We are free to exercise relentless pursuit of anything we deeply believe or desire.

If individuals become discouraged, something entirely different may be happening. Perhaps people feel low energy levels, and a shift needs to take place—but don't give up.

Moods are like people's internal weather barometers. When people experience low moods, they gravitate toward and focus on problems; people experience a heightened but distorted sense of immediacy; they may feel self-absorbed and don't focus on solutions. When individuals experience a negative attitude and demeanor, they are accompanied by negative thoughts, emotions, and outcomes.

Never accept defeat. Check in with yourself on the physical, mental, emotional, and spiritual level and see where you are out of balance. The experience of well-being or feeling congruent occurs when these four levels are balanced and aligned. When an individual experiences feeling discouraged, it is likely that one of these levels is out of alignment. Gently check in, go inside, and makes some inquiries. Are you hungry? Do you need exercise? Is something bothering you emotionally? Are you sad or angry? Do you need to rest? Are you bored or angry? Could you use a power nap? Would some self-care, like a therapeutic massage, help? Would a twenty-minute spiritual meditation re-center you?

Awakened leaders insist that people are the most important assets. The tendency to give up or give in is associated with fatigue and low energy. People are far more effective to others when they are tuned up. So tune up, don't give up; never defer to defeat.

People must honor their bodies and administer self-care for their mind and spirit to thrive. Many of us were taught and conditioned as children that "selfishness" is wrong or indulgent. The reverse is true; only by taking proper care of ourselves can we be available, accessible, and serve others. Self-care decisions are not "selfish;" they are self-nurturing, self-honoring and self-assuring.

As leaders, we have choices to recharge and regroup as well. People prefer to encounter leaders who are balanced, cheerful, accessible, alert and empathic people-in-charge. Envision yourselves in that role, in that setting. Become calm, fit, generous, energetic, and compassionate leaders.

Leaders get no points for being martyrs or victims. People's responsibility lies with themselves. Allowing anything less is deleterious to the organization and the people that the leader serves. Leaders' self-care benefits all people.

In my experience, when I take excellent care of myself, I am more available, I listen more attentively, and I am more emotionally accessible. When I am centered, I enjoy being with others and interacting with them both on a personal and a professional level.

Effective leaders set an example, take excellent care of themselves on all levels, and create business environments and policies that promote and encourage employees' self-care. Leaders always monitor their internal barometers to adjust and align themselves. Leaders never accept defeat.

Principle 47

Play Large

Our greatest fear is not that we are inadequate. Our deepest fear is that we are powerful beyond measure. It is our light, not our darkness, that frightens us.

—Marianne Williamson
Author of *A Return to Love*

Accepting that you can't control the outcome is not the end of action. You can accept total responsibility for your choices and achieve. You are free to play full out in creation and implementing an extraordinary future for yourself and your organization.

—Tracy Goss
Author of *The Last Word on Power*

You do not belong to you. You belong to the universe.

—Buckminster Fuller (1895-1983)
Architect, author, poet,
inventor–patented the geodesic dome

Sooner or later, many individuals will tire of staying small or playing it safe. Many people simply desire to leave the world a better place. Leaders hold their positions in large part because they rarely played small, and they definitely desired to forge a legacy that served a large audience.

Leaders continually endeavor to exceed their upper limit. This may involve learning new skills, developing new talents, gathering expertise in new areas, and assessing and taking risks. Much of this process is people's inner journey to find and discover their purpose. Coaching has often been described as guiding people to express the life of their dreams. Leaders often employ coaches to improve themselves, their people, and their business plans.

Playing large often means offering yourself to others in service. Leaders often extend themselves in service, both in their company and within their community. They serve on boards of directors; work as volunteer advisors to leaders of philanthropic, cultural, and non-profit organizations; educate youth and mentor teens. They lend their names to raise funds for charitable causes that benefit those in need.

In my experience, incredibly gratifying things happen when I volunteer my time and experience. I have less spare time, yet I endeavor and accomplish more, with grace and ease. As synchronicity works for the highest good, I meet like-minded, like-hearted people in the process. Service work has become my passion.

When individuals decide to play large, they stretch themselves through a series of committed action steps. At each level, they create a new way of being. Their ability to contribute to others and serve others grows immeasurably. They become inherently focused on others as they put forth effort, exercise creation, and expand. There is truth in the concept that the more people give, the more they receive. But I invite you to experience it for yourself.

My experience teaching, supporting, and coaching others is pure joy. Supportive inquiry and centered listening often reveal what clients may not see for themselves. The satisfaction I experience in mentoring and guiding clients to express their own inner greatness is immeasurable. Playing large benefits everyone.

Principle 48

Evaluate Performance Using Two-Way Communication

In the last analysis, our only freedom is the freedom to discipline ourselves.
—Bernard Baruch (1870-1965)

Performance evaluations often seem like one-way conversations. Supervisors or leaders often complete performance appraisals indicating tasks and projects that were well done and suggest areas that could be improved.

In my experience, I recall that many of the performance benchmarks were situational. They occurred as organizations grew and changed. I have often felt separate from circumstantial performance criteria. I believe a better way would be to have both parties own their part in facilitating the changes, reaching performance goals, and communicating how they respectively might contribute to increased results.

An effective business relationship requires contribution and communication from both people. Supervisors and leaders can greatly benefit from their people's suggestions or feedback. Employees may have ideas for process, procedure, work product, or output improvement. Synergy and support result when both people communicate and participate.

At times of rapid change within companies, effective bottom-up communication is very valuable for both the leaders and the company. Often the employees with the most knowledge about process improvement are the people who perform the work. They are experts who think about their work, their procedure, and how best to achieve goals and objectives each workday. The workers and the organization itself benefit when they are involved in the work design and process improvements.

If performance assessments are conducted well, they may be utilized as powerful motivational sessions. An effective leader knows his people, and a key motivational skill is awakening what is already in a person. Leadership actually brings out untapped potential through careful inquiry, supportive questioning, well-timed interventions, and caring facilitation. Motivation should be the spine of the evaluation process, which seeks refinement of any fashion.

In many of today's information-based organizations, operational models have been effectively redesigned around team development and deployment. They are composed of knowledge workers. Multiple teams of specialists complete projects or elements of projects. More collaboration and feedback occur in this project model. Particularly in project-based environments, two-way communication improves as individuals are given a voice on their project team and evaluated with the same two-way approach. All workers benefit from improved information exchange and communication and a mutual dialogue in performance reviews.

Principle 49

Monitor Mood and Choose Attitude

Always think of what you have to do as easy, and it will be.
—Emile Coue, psychologist and philosopher

Nothing has any meaning until we assign it meaning; nothing in the workplace does either.
—Steve Chandler

Human beings have far more mastery over their attitude when they understand that attitude is a choice. This is because feelings come from thoughts. We have the ability to alter our feelings when we change our thought consciously. It may require some facilitation from a trainer or a coach, but when individuals become skilled at monitoring attitude from within, performance can soar. One could say that mood is the background that supports attitude in the foreground.

People prolong moods by indulging in certain types of thinking and perceiving how they are feeling. Moods are states that determine our energy. Moods involve biochemistry and are colored by our memory of past events. I like to think of moods as the backdrop of people's thoughts and feelings. They have a great deal of influence on how we perceive life. When our mood is low, we become insecure and that reduces our creativity. George Pransky has written, "Moods are the constant shifts in perspective built into our experience of life. Our thinking and therefore our perceptions of life are a function of mood changes. Our thoughts are more optimistic, light-hearted, and wise when we are in a high mood."

People's low moods often distort their natural experience of life. They negatively interpret events that they may otherwise view from a neutral position. People in low moods receive faulty information from their brains. Low moods are heavy, serious, and laced with urgency and conditioned thought. They are altered states of consciousness because our natural state is one of well-being. Experienced leaders have long recognized that the majority of conflicts occur when people experience low moods.

When leaders adopt understanding attitudes, they transform energies from conflict to willingness. Energetic leaders raise people's energy. High-energy moods produce expansive and creative thoughts that seem vast and timeless.

Leaders understand that the work environment is often the genesis of attitude. When workers are supported and encouraged, the mind is positively influenced to produce beneficial attitudes with which to promote achievement and success. That is why leadership contributes so much to a positive cultural environment where heightened attitudes are the norm.

Leaders' own attitudes carry great influence as they guide people and organizations. Leaders' roles involve communicating clear messages and conveying ideas. These messages express who they are as people and creators. One could say that the leaders' attitudes affect the entire direction of organizations because they affect the attitudes of others.

Because moods and attitudes are so interconnected, attitude becomes a steering wheel of sorts, for our sense of well-being. We choose our personal reality through perception. The power is in the choice because we have the ability to program our mind to produce what we desire.

Attitude shift is actually a shift in perception. An energetic attitude influences the outcome we attract and enhances the lives we create. Heightening our attitude becomes very gratifying when we realize the genuine influence we actually wield over what we create and experience. Attitudes hold amazing potency and carry great potential for individuals to create through committed engagement.

Principle 50

Seek Agreement and Soften Differences

Problems are never solved on the same level in which they were created.

—Albert Einstein

Individuals have different perceptions of reality so each of us holds different viewpoints of the world and its events. So they are only opinions—100% of the time! When individuals look for disagreement, it can be a subtle, destructive habit that erodes the spirit of cooperation.

Effective leaders are good negotiators; they are optimists and seek agreement. They embrace neutrality as openness and strength. Skilled negotiation releases the resistance and judgment of the opposing position and considers it. Often, conclusion is reached when the opposite is accepted or incorporated. Neutral means neutral, by playing for a win-win outcome.

With respect to internal business dialogue, leaders know that disagreement de-motivates and undermines people's efforts. It throws people off balance. Excessive disagreement furthers defensiveness, divisiveness, and discord. The atmosphere dampens communication when it is perceived that agreement is a futile endeavor. Disagreement produces antagonism; agreement fosters teamwork, bonding, energy, and motivation.

Effective leaders acknowledge that no greater method exists to reinforce and reassure people than to find agreement with them. Agreement acknowledges them and builds trust and rapport. Leaders assuage differences and seek agreement to further communication among their people. People who interact with effective leaders feel heard, valued, and supported.

Leaders listen for the value in what people say and express. Sincere leaders set the tone in meetings by looking for agreement. They dramatically influence the meetings' outcome because they actively encourage people's participation. People feel that their involvement adds value. There is nothing wrong with parsing views, debating opinions, or vetting issues. But how leaders foster communication to encourage participation, respect, and agreement on sometimes-differing issues is crucial.

Communicative leaders look for agreement and work toward consensus to strengthen relationships. Agreement serves and benefits internal and external relationships.

Principle 51

Elevate with Humor and Laughter

Laughter is the shortest distance between two people.
—Victor Borge, Musician, humorist

I've always thought that a big laugh is a really loud noise from the soul saying, "Ain't that the truth."
—Quincy Jones

The leadership you are born with is the backbone. Then you develop the funny bone and the wishbone that go with it.
—Elaine Agather, CEO, JP Morgan Chase

Leaders have the ability to laugh with themselves and enjoy humor. They appreciate that it is impossible to be upset or stressed out about anything when one laughs. There is great tension release in laughter. The reason is simple: *it is impossible to be worried about the past or stressed about the assumed future when we laugh.* When we laugh, we are totally in the present moment, in joy. It is literally impossible to experience negativity, fear, anger, or hostility of any kind during laughter. Laughter is elated and joyful.

During a leadership conference that I attended, the keynote speaker asked the audience, "What is the greatest stress reliever?" Participants' replies included exercise, food, meditation, playing with pets, rest, alcohol, sleep, reading, time spent with family, sex, time in nature, etc. What was incredible was that **not one *person* gave the correct answer, which is laughter**.

Laughter is the most effective stress breaker in this world. Laughter is instantaneous, spontaneous, and free. It comes in unlimited supply, and it works every time. Laughter bonds people together and helps them see clearly, without emotional anchors. It assists them in communicating effectively.

When humor and laughter are prevalent in the business environment, they elevate everyone. They are the essence of good cheer and business relations.

Principle 52

Lead from the Inside Out

If you focus on principles, you empower everyone who understands those principles to act without constant monitoring, evaluating, correcting or controlling.
—Stephen R. Covey

Be the change you wish to see in the world.
—Gandhi

Be a leader. Your being-ness *is* your leadership.

People respond to your essence as a leader. If a leader's power is authentic, people believe in the leader and his message. People demonstrate that they believe in their leaders when they follow. They follow where a leader's principles, values, and actions enact outcomes for the greater good.

People trust and emulate leaders whom they respect. People respect what leaders represent and what leaders mean to them. Leaders serve as living examples and role models. Their leadership is a presence that is felt. That essence is authentic leadership.

Leaders transform organizations by exhibiting forthright and steadfast leadership. The transformation starts within. Lead from the inside out.

Principle 53

Look Good Authentically

Because he believes in himself, he does not need to convince others. Because he is content with himself, he doesn't need the other's approval. Because he accepts himself, the whole world accepts him.

—The Tao Te Ching

There's a colloquial expression that states: "Management is doing things right. Leadership is doing the right thing." Catering to appearance is insincere and actually the opposite of authentic leadership. No matter how subtle the "looking good," worker teams notice the insincerity and people become uncomfortable. As leaders, we do not want to send a message that says, "I am more concerned about how I look to my peers than in doing what is right."

Seeking approval focuses upon external appearance rather than internal confidence. If people in positions of leadership feel that they are "not quite enough," they unconsciously express a need for approval from others. That process does not support healthy self-esteem. Great leaders are not motivated by what "looks good" to gain attention and adulation.

Pandering to appearance is not authentic leadership because it is not based on anything real. When we are seeking approval and appreciation, it is because we are feeling insecure. There is always more fulfillment in being a loving presence, rather than seeking it. Authenticity is drawn from within

We could name this skill *choosing emotional independence*: How others perceive me or what they choose, has nothing to do with who I am. They might act the same even if I weren't here. Another viewpoint is, when you are engaged doing the right thing, that action will ensure personal advancement, because it contains integrity. In conscious leadership, you also advance the good of all.

Eventually, all leaders will face difficult, complex decisions. Effective leaders embrace the complexity and choose the correct course. Authentic intuition often plays a role.

Authentic leadership stems from a solid sense of knowing the self. Authentic leaders pursue mitigating risk and resolving challenge with the conscious wisdom of what is best, never upon appearance.

Principle 54

Transform Worry into Puzzle Solving

Greatness is not a function of circumstance. Greatness ... is a matter of conscious choice.

—Jim Collins
Author of *Good to Great*

If people's response to their challenges is worry, they reduce and diffuse their focus and intention. Worry responses lower their energy and erode their confidence.

Choosing to worry is hardly a self-empowering action, and there is a better way to manage work process and flow. Reframe the approach, upgrade the problem transforming it into a challenge, and create an action plan to better address the issue and solve the problem.

Reframing involves developing a new view about how we conceive a problem as a challenge or even or a puzzle to be solved. It can actually be fun, uplifting, and rewarding to sort out pieces and issues and accede them. And breaking the challenge down into pieces really helps. Accepting a challenge with high motivation is a great use of energy and creativity. Staying in a worry state with its cousins—anxiety, fear, and doubt—drains people's imaginations, the very source of their energy and creativity.

Leaders and coaches, by their nature, seek to widen perspective and increase choices and options. Challenges reframed as a puzzle can be engaging and interesting to solve. Worry never solves the puzzle.

Principle 55

Balance Technology with Humanity

He is advancing in life whose heart is getting softer, his brain quicker and his spirit entering into living Peace
—John Ruskin (1819-1900)
Author, poet, artist, art critic

Effective leaders guide people and create supportive business environments. Leaders who practice kindness and demonstrate genuine concern for people's welfare encourage phenomenal performance. The kindness that emanates from leaders permeates the entire culture of an organization.

Downsizing and increased technology in business settings have contributed to the modern, stressful business environment. While high performance, accuracy, skilled execution, and excellence have always been key attributes of successful organizations, turnaround time has been dramatically reduced.

Many people are racing to keep up with laptops, cell phones, e-mail, hand-held computers, instant text messaging, large PDF files, and other real-time communication systems. These continual stimuli tax the human mind with constant new input. Because of mobile communication devices, people sometimes feel that they are never "off duty". Workers often feel subjugated to an electronic work life of ministering to fast-track, multiple deadlines while many different communication devices compete for their time and attention. The expectation of reacting constantly to the pace set by technology leads to burnout and ultimately to lowered productivity.

Workers deserve adequate time to focus, digest, and process information to make quality decisions. As people experience information overload, they have a tendency to become less accessible. People starved of time and energy cannot produce optimal results even with technological efficiencies.

While information technology creates many back-end efficiencies, human planning and quality execution must be preserved on the front end. Leaders who create supportive business cultures eliminate an undercurrent of people pitted against the speed of technology and reactive responses. These electronic efficiencies must not replace creative human planning and the power of inspired human thought.

Leaders employ a potent antidote for workplace stress when they create compassionate, supportive business cultures. Understanding support from leaders and colleagues balances the potentially impersonal nature of today's business. People feel valued and remain energetic and creative as they receive genuine consideration. Encouragement and care sustain the human soul in the workplace of automation and technology.

Caring leaders are not misled into thinking that the work output itself is more important than the ongoing value of the people who perform that work. While leaders need to monitor processes, systems, productivity, and profit, great leaders acknowledge and appreciate people. They understand that people are the very source of production. Leaders who promulgate a kind business culture provide an effective antidote to stress created by technological advances in modern business environments.

The meaning of the phrase, "It's lonely at the top," has always eluded me. Most leaders I have known are warm, accessible, balanced, cheerful, and amiable. They are genuinely interested in their people's well-being. Leaders who create supportive, nurturing business cultures contribute substantially to productivity alongside technology.

Principle 56

Cherish Children, Strengthen Community

If we are to have peace in the world, it begins with the children.
—Gandhi

Each new child seems to be sufficient reason for the whole universe's being set in motion...and what the end of it will be is still very much an open question.
—Thornton Wilder, playwright

Children reflect and embody human potential. They represent the entire future of the global village.

Compassionate leaders acknowledge the important role families and children play in employees' lives. Life and livelihood are intertwined, and it is a challenge for many people to maintain balance between their personal and professional lives.

Leaders have opportunities to deeply relate to employees through the concern leaders show for families. In strengthening the company culture, conscious leaders transform the organization into a community of sorts. In turn, business communities care for their most basic of all communities—the family.

There also exists opportunities for leaders and businesses to become involved with the community they serve. Leaders and businesses can support organizations that assist children and families.

Community outreach resonates with and catalyzes workers because people love to mentor and assist children. Volunteers become highly engaged because workers adore children and find the outreach so rewarding. It energizes employees, families, and communities and re-kindles their passion and zeal.

When businesses perform charitable works for any children, especially under-privileged or economically challenged children, people align with the heart of the business in community service.

Those of us who work with youth know that few activities could be more rewarding or more powerful. Simply look into the face of a joyful, grateful child and you will observe love of life itself. Working with kids brings out the best in us; it creates a deep sense of purpose. When that love of children runs collectively through the business organization, it strengthens the bonds between people like no other activity.

Principle 57

You Never Outgrow Your Need for Mentors

Our chief want in life is to find someone who will make us do what we can.
—Ralph Waldo Emerson

Coaching rests on the premise that the client possesses unrecognized resources with which he or she can develop strategies that lead aspirations to their fulfillment; the focus is on the present and the future. It's about putting the client in touch with his or her own wisdom and creativity. Coaching looks to close the gap between our dreams and the realities of our existence.

—Nathaniel Branden
Psychologist, Author, &
Founder of *The Institute for Self-Esteem*

Coaching in business is effective and powerful. Why? Because it originated in the world of sports, an industry of performance and numbers. Businesses also want to improve numbers, advance their teams, and achieve proactive success through vision and playing the game well. Sport coaching is a great metaphor for what effective coaching can do for business organizations and their leaders.

Leaders who read this book are sincerely encouraged to consider hiring and maintaining an executive coach or life coach. Even the finest coaches in the industry retain a coach. My personal coach, Steve Chandler, has a superb coach, Steve Hardison, who is one of the "greats." Coaching assists leaders in achieving continual expansion of their perspective and skills. Coaches ensure that their talents are allowed to emerge, refining their leadership abilities and allowing them to be in harmony with their personal and professional aspirations.

Coaching gives leaders an infinitely broader perspective to create more inspired choices and options. Effective coaches can often identify potential within leaders that may be missed in the busy pace of business. Coaches work as inspirational sounding boards for the client's inner world. They also support leaders in navigating the vagaries of the outer world.

Coaches bring forth the greatness within leaders. Skilled coaches facilitate through supportive inquiry and well-timed interventions. They illuminate personal discovery. Coaching stretches leaders beyond their current upper limit and assists them in transcending any perceived obstacle or challenge. I like to call coaching "leadership alchemy" because coaches provide a blueprint of who we can be. Leaders possess many powerful talents that are enhanced when drawn forth by coaching. A skilled coach facilitates an "envisioned future" of the clients, creating with them the life of their own invention.

Through their own coaching, conscious leaders become effective mentors. Leaders coach their leadership teams to higher potential and greater success. They move their organizations forward, like sports teams, by improving playing skills, increasing the numbers, and advancing the mission.

Recent surveys indicate that over seventy percent of today's business leaders receive mentoring and guidance from an executive coach to ensure their professional success and personal fulfillment. Leaders achieve much more than they could possibly achieve on their own. Great athletes, actors, dancers, musicians, and performers all utilize coaches. So do good leaders.

Principle 58

Conduct Great Meetings Every Time

Plans are worthless, but planning is invaluable.
—Peter Drucker

Meetings without well-defined purpose and focus only serve to waste time and erode staff morale. Meetings ideally should be stimulating, relevant, educational or topic-centered, and timely. This also applies to recurring informational meetings like production meetings and personnel training.

To ensure that your meetings have organized content, structure, and well-prepared topics, *provide a printed agenda.* A written agenda signals to participants that the meeting is important, well thought out, and carefully planned. It also sends a clear signal that the leader is prepared to lead the meeting.

Here are my "12 Commandments" for ensuring successful meetings:

1. Hold meetings at a time when people are alert and attentive. Avoid planning meetings late in the day when most people's energy is lower.

2. Offer at least one five-minute break so participants can stretch, refill coffee, have a quick snack and/or use the facilities. People appreciate breaks that honor their bodies, minds, and boundaries.

3. Hold meetings in rooms with adequate light and good ventilation or adequate air-conditioning. Stuffy rooms with stale air do not assist participants to stay alert when they must sit stationary for long periods of time.

4. Host the meeting off site when possible—even at a coffee shop or restaurant—which provides a change of scenery. This contributes to making attendees feel valued.

5. When meetings take place on site, close conference-room doors and do not encourage interruptions from other managers, other departments, and/or operating divisions. If you set the tone that your meeting has importance, others will regard it as important.

6. Always open the meeting with a greeting and "checking-in" session with the attendees. Proceeding right into the first meeting topic is impersonal—"tech" without "touch." It honors the attendees to ask how they are and builds rapport with the meeting leader.

7. Introduce humor and fun when appropriate. Humor gratifies and entertains people and leaders, alike when they know that meetings are not all serious business. Meetings with an overly serious tone can lower morale. People appreciate being treated as honored participants. They respond positively to lightness and humor.

8. Use more than one meeting leader and time if multiple topics are presented. Doing so sets a pace and tone for each segment of the meeting. For instance, four one-hour training meetings on the same day are more effective than one four-hour

meeting. Participants can absorb and retain more information.

9. Serve refreshments. Providing complimentary coffee, tea, mineral water, other beverages, fruit, and healthy snacks makes people feel appreciated.

10. Don't rely solely on PowerPoint presentations. Overhead slides are great for information sharing, but meeting leaders should make time for dialogue and commentary. There is more balance when data and statistics are blended with live communication. Blend technology with humanity.

11. Provide time for questions and answers, particularly when presenting new material.

12. Complete the meeting the same way you began, with a personal checking-in segment. For example, ask attendees for take-away insights, such as what they learned, what they liked, what could be presented better or differently in the future. It refocuses the attendees, summarizes the content, and gives very valuable feedback to the meeting leader. When meeting attendees are offered a forum where they can express themselves, relationships deepen, morale increases, and motivation for the next meeting is put in place.

Principle 59

Language Is Leadership

The leader works in the open, and the boss in covert. The leader leads and the boss drives.

—Theodore Roosevelt

In leadership we communicate the team vision. We also show ourselves. Leaders communicate; that is their main job. A simple act can say much about the leader because leadership manifests in what and how we communicate.

Therefore, good leaders strive to articulate in a style befitting a leader. Leaders strive to use correct grammar and professional language in all business settings. This applies to both spoken dialogue and written communications.

Clear thinking and good communication go hand in hand. Speak and write in an appropriate manner that leaves little room for error, misunderstanding, or misperception. Communication from a leader contains clear content and contextual meaning. Effective communication defines the manner befitting a leader.

I believe that communication from a leader should represent education, refinement, and goodwill. Individuals in positions of leadership set high standards through communication. That standard becomes emblematic for the communication and leadership articulation throughout the organization, especially for supervisors and managers. Quality communication becomes a fabric of the culture.

Effective use of language is a demonstrated skill of leadership. Every business communication from the leader is both a symbol of leadership and an opportunity to produce a positive impact on the entire business organization.

Principle 60

Create a Disciplined Routine

Discipline is remembering what you want.
—David Campbell,
founder of Saks Fifth Avenue

The victory of success is half won when one gains the habit of setting goals and achieving them. Even the most tedious chore will become endurable as you parade through each day convinced that every task, no matter how menial or boring, brings you closer to fulfilling your dreams.
—Og Mandino, (1923-1996)
Author and motivational speaker

When workers worry as to where to focus their time, energy, and effort, they do not have a disciplined routine. When individuals seem fragmented or less than purposeful, it's not because they are flawed or unworthy. They simply lack a disciplined routine. With a purposeful routine, they begin to demonstrate effective activity and achievement. A disciplined routine puts a structure around endeavor and gives purpose and objective goals to chosen activity.

The word *discipline* comes from the word *disciple*. Disciples are devoted to a cause or goal. They make efforts, take actions, and are willing to explore and learn.

In *Principle-Centered Leadership*, Stephen Covey presents a great metaphor. He compares business to a "farm model". He explains that anything business people wish to harvest must first be cultivated like soil for crops. Soil is prepared, tilled, fertilized, and watered. Only then does one reap the harvest.

I love the wisdom saying which states that, it is easy to overestimate what can be done in a day, (or week) and very easy to underestimate what can be done in a year. A discipline with a routine, over time, can accomplish phenomenal results.

Leaders have a wonderful opportunity to teach that effort, combined with an organized routine, is very powerful. Disciplined routine allows an achiever to do the job in an excellent way, to stay productively busy, and to stop worrying.

Principle 61

Internalize Courage as Choice

It takes a lot of courage to release the familiar and seemingly secure, to embrace the new. But there is no real security in what is no longer meaningful. There is more security in the adventurous and exciting, for in movement there is life, and in change there is power.

—Alan Cohen

Often the greatest fear leads to the greatest freedom. Reality is not our enemy; the universe is kind.

—Byron Katie
Author of *Loving What Is*

Leadership ability is developed over periods of years. With increasing levels of mastery, leaders refine their skill, build confidence and competence, and embrace courage in the process. Through my research and personal journey, I have discovered that *leadership* has many levels of meaning. The quality we call courage allows us to access the advanced levels of leadership and conscious living.

What often gives people difficulty transitioning to their next level of success is simply an imagined barrier. Most of us measure the creative potential for the future, by what was feasible in the past. That is the source of limiting beliefs. What separates people from having that new, desired existence and quality of life are only limiting thoughts that are believed.

Courage is the choice to investigate those thoughts, to challenge the beliefs that limit our action, and to change the internal script. Courage is making the choice to create a new perspective. Courage is an ever-present choice point because it is the threshold of conscious shift. Courage is an internal coming-out.

There is a mystical relationship between fear and courage. In my experience, when internal shifts are embraced, there is often accompanying fear or even terror. We may be filled with doubt, anxiety or confusion. We are given the choice to inquire of our thoughts, examine what we choose to believe, and initiate new action. With conscious choice, we are free from believing thoughts from the past. When fear is present, we have the opportunity to transcend it. By meeting our thoughts with understanding, we access our internal compass of truth, our own source. Courage is choosing anew.

Courage is not something genetic with which we are born. Courage is not a quality that anyone possesses or a character trait. Courage is creation, a choice that transcends fear. Courage can be accessed by anyone, or not, by self-honoring choice. We can choose creation in any moment when we choose to transcend fear and mobilize our new choice into action. Courage is always the choice for freedom, in the name of peace. Courage, as creation, is the foundational wisdom that "transformation starts from within."

Principle 62

Enjoy Gifted Friends and Great Books

A good book is like an old friend.
—Anonymous

I once heard a superb executive trainer declare: *"The two greatest influences of your life after high school or college are the company you keep and the books you read."* That remark has remained and resonated with me for years. I attribute the vast majority of my experience, growth, and learning to certain influential people and many inspiring books. Books are the expressions of gifted people who choose to write about their subjects of mastery and share their experience with others.

Leaders use discernment to choose companions of like mind and like heart; they unite in common interests and common causes. A genuine energetic connection is often spawned by the community of minds. Effective leaders leverage many minds to develop strong relationships and forge alliances to tap into the collective creativity and intelligence of people. This may include professionals from across their business and industry through a trade association. Community organizations are another rich source for regional resources, as well as other businesses and their leaders.

Most leaders who I know read a great deal of literature on business, global markets, and leadership and management practices. Reading good books offers

challenging opportunities for continuous learning as
well as being well rounded. Books broaden leaders'
perspectives and life influences. Many published
authors are experts in their respective field. This
includes books on management or marketing in which
authors share their experience of success. A vast array
of books on any imaginable topic exists today. Rich
assortments of books are available in multiple forms as
well. Electronic, audio and written formats expand
people's options. Books can now be directly
downloaded from the Internet as well.

Leaders avail themselves of all types of people,
knowledge and available information to stay informed.
They enrich their thinking from a collective mind of
expertise found in the resources of both people and
good literature.

Principle 63

Nurture Yourself

This above all else, to thine own self be true.

—William Shakespeare

Sometimes we treat ourselves as machines that need refueling rather than as living beings who have natural rhythms of our own. Look closely at the root of the word recreation, *re-creating*. Nurturing and recreation indicates a frame of mind for doing something "just for the fun of doing it," (not to achieve anything). Like children, who know how to play, we need to do something essential for good mental health. This is our time of "Re-creation."

In *The Power of Full Engagement*, Tony Schwartz and Jim Loehr present case studies of burned-out business executives with whom they worked to assist in living more balanced, effective lives. The central focus of their work is managing energy.

They often improved upon a client's nutrition by recommending healthier food choices. They created regular exercise regimens for other clients. Sometimes they created a reframing of how they held family time as a joy rather than a burden or responsibility. Even little things like a 20-minute "power nap" or a quick walk in the park after lunch can keep leaders in tune with nature and themselves.

A familiar theme in the modern business world is making time for important things. This includes "quality" thinking time and self-nurturing.

We often hear the phrase, "Take care of yourself." Do you? When leaders are balanced, it means that they are congruent physically, mentally, emotionally, and spiritually. Leaders are at their best when they provide for themselves on all these levels. They know the importance of sustaining balance with health, business, and family. I like to call it providing for life, living, and livelihood.

To maintain ourselves as energetic, enthusiastic leaders, we must first be balanced human beings. Mind, body, and spirit are all important.

Here is one way that I learned that works well to provide time for self-care within a busy, heavily scheduled life: plan in advance. Put specific activities in writing. Put scheduled times for exercise, eating, recreation, and planning on your calendar/planner—and adhere to them faithfully.

Compose a "fun and joy" list that uniquely suits your interests and meets your needs. These activities are self-nurturing, enjoyable, and regenerative. Then commit to participate in at least two "fun and joy" activities per week.

You could write such things as:

"Walk on the beach." "Take a brisk walk in a beautiful park." "Enjoy a hike in the mountains or desert." "Host a gourmet picnic." "Take a day trip to the village." "Treat myself to a massage." "Go shopping at my favorite boutique." "Play nine holes of golf." "Swim 30 laps in the pool." "Spend quality time with a beloved pet." "Take a tennis lesson."

There are many possibilities. What are your favorite activities? Having adequate time for enjoyment is vital to physical, mental, and emotional fitness and balance.

It's simple and effective if you commit at least twice weekly for your well-being. Items on your "fun and joy" list become upper-priority activities for self-renewal. The activities can assist you and sustain you physically and spiritually. Give yourself the care you deserve. You are the most important person you know. When practiced regularly, self-nurturing activities become self-honoring, restorative habits.

Who else is most deserving of your kindness and nurturing? No one. You'll be more balanced and congruent. Make your "fun and joy" list, and people will notice the difference.

Principle 64

Lead with the **Right Brain** and **Manage** with the **Left Brain**

You can't depend on your judgment when your imagination is out of focus.
—Mark Twain

We live subject to arrest by degrees of fatigue which we have come only from habit to obey. Most of us can learn to live in perfect comfort on much higher levels of power.
—William James

The two hemispheres of the brain serve us through distinctly different functions. They serve us like two vast operating systems within a computer.

The left brain has often been called the *guardian brain*. The left hemisphere is concerned with analytics and is also the source of urgency because of its concern for time and space. Some researchers have stated that the left hemisphere acts as a filter to prevent too many stimuli, keeping us balanced and sane; it is the "vigilant" brain. The left brain examines solutions, options, and choices. The left brain looks *outward* upon the world. The left brain observes content.

The right hemisphere has been called the *door to wisdom* and focuses on the creative and the conceptual, that which has not yet been brought into being. Right-brain creativity assists in procreating our desires through envisioning and inventing our future. The right brain looks *inward* for meaning and conceptual reality. The right brain observes context.

Leaders are primarily responsible for creating the future of their organizations. Their vision originates within the right hemisphere and then manifests through planning within the left hemisphere, which addresses the world of time and space.

Imagination is the powerful source of creation and energy. The right brain imagines concepts, which is beyond time and space, from a magnificent source within. That is the world of imagination, the source of motivation where dreams become reality. Leaders whose thought impulses flow between both hemispheres process thought neither solely through "worldly" analysis (mostly pattern recognition), nor solely through creative invention, without worldly discipline. Hence the directive, "lead with the right and manage with the left."

Both brain functions serve as valuable information resources for leaders. Leaders exceed the limits of habitual thinking, which is the protection mechanism of the left brain. Utilizing dual brain functions supports leaders in confronting ambiguity and vagary in the realm of decision making. Leaders find resourceful thought by "mining" both levels of thought. Harnessing the resources of both big-picture thinking and rigorous attention to detail supports the dual processes of leadership and management well. Worldly content combines with contextual wisdom to process substantive knowledge, the heart of all decision making and good leadership.

Principle 65

Take Decisive Action

The reasons CEOs are the most important people in the organization is because they can choose to make things happen. I think the perspective of being the one in the hot seat, so to speak, is extremely valuable.
—Steve Chandler

Effective leadership is composed of making internal declarations and then creating an effective plan of execution. It is the leader's ability to build a bridge between probability and reality, from a vision through to a plan of action. Leaders investigate alternatives, explore an array of options, refine issues, and apply objectivity to the choices at hand. But all good planning becomes a plan of action. Commitment to an action plan becomes a unique kind of certainty.

The leader's vision becomes the future of the company. The leader creates a space for the not yet achieved to be achieved. One could think of the leadership vision as a created reality, which is brought forth into actuality through committed action steps.

Many leaders choose to inculcate their vision, powerfully, into the organization through making declarations. Thus, the imagined reality becomes supported by the declaration of what is achievable. An example declaration statement could read: "The competitive edge for my company is my people; they are the most important resource." When leaders take an emboldened stand, make a declaration that is practiced as a living vision and not a rhetorical slogan, it becomes the principle design for the company and its future.

Making declarations and taking decisive action from a realm of possibility always moves the possibility forward. It is transformative leadership in motion. Leaders propel the vision through committed action plans. Planning and execution, vision and action are where the rubber meets the road.

Principle 66

Go Within

Inquiry is where we meet our thoughts with understanding.
—Byron Katie
Author of *Loving What Is*

Nothing shapes our lives as much as the questions we ask, or refuse to ask, throughout our lives.
—Richard J. Leider
Author of *The Power of Purpose*

Conventional knowledge says that people often receive their best ideas either during a shower or when they are on vacation. Why? People in the shower or who are on vacation have slowed down and have accessed a different level of the mind.

Invention and productivity are always created spontaneously, in the present moment. When the mind is not focused on disappointments of the past or anxiety about the future, the higher level of our creative mind is "allowed" to emerge from within. When we quiet the mind, ingenuity can come forth.

A rapid pace often accompanies contemporary living. Some individuals find that it is difficult to unwind from constant activity and mental processing. Modern psychologists have observed that subtle fear often accompanies periods of not being busy. Yet, constant activity impedes the creative mind.

There is always the possibility of incorporating new knowledge or wisdom without the chatter of the rational mind.

For creative thinking, often the best remedy is to slow down and to go within. To go within is to trust, to ask questions and access that creative mind which is the source of ingenuity. Such a mind is open to imagination and new possibilities. That is a mind open to inquiry.

Deep knowing can be imparted experientially to leaders as insight and intuition. When we enter the quiet, we are ready to listen. When we go within, we are ready to receive.

Principle 67

Encourage Organizational Learning

With the eyes of ignorance we can only see a short distance and think there is nothing beyond. We need a discriminating intellect that distinguishes between truth and untruth. Awareness is the most important act of all.
—Ammachi, known as the "hugging saint," Kerala, India

Stephen Covey states that great leaders are the ones who seek "true north." They innovate with many methods and in many ways. They seek new methods, processes, technology, manufacturing techniques, delivery systems, procedures and prospective markets. Leaders continually adapt systems through change and refinement. Most important, the innovation is shared within the organization as continuous learning.

Adopting a continual learning orientation is important in today's rapidly evolving global economy. Organizations are adapting faster than at any time in previous history. Organizational leadership and knowledge must evolve rapidly, through learning, to keep abreast of innovation and global change.

In today's knowledge-based organizations, often the genesis of new ideas is the workers, themselves, who innovate through many incremental improvements. In *Good to Great*, Jim Collins suggests that "continuous learning organization" is one of the key drivers of organizations that succeed and excel to become the leaders in their industries. Leaders have a choice to either stay "good" and eventually decay or to learn and become great.

If the business organization embraces a continual learning orientation, the culture fosters innovation. The company encourages and supports people to continually experiment and grow. Learning also challenges people and allows them to advance into new levels of expertise. Learning also can serve as a tool for employee retention because workers feel valued.

Learning also creates a motivated environment where people thrive and expand. They may begin to compete with each another to create and produce in new ways.

There's an axiom that there are no mistakes, only new learning. Leaders who encourage education, experimentation, and innovation create an adventurous culture where individuals thrive and the organization keeps pace with global business change.

Principle 68

Tithe and Give Back

There is no difference between giving and receiving.
—*A Course in Miracles*

We must raise the threshold of our awareness so that we could see ourselves for what we really are: individual cells in the immortal body of humanity.
—Dr. Norman Cousins
Author of *Anatomy of an Illness*

Every ancient spiritual tradition was consistent in teaching the principle of contribution and generosity through giving. They taught expressing compassion through charitable works, service to others, and tithing a proportion of one's income or earnings. This teaching embodied generosity of spirit as a personal virtue.

There is a large movement today toward "for-profit" philanthropy and companies that call themselves "philanthro-preneurial", as they exist to do good while doing well. Tithing encompasses the universal principle of giving and receiving. When businesses make substantial profits and allocate portions to assist people, that action bonds people in good will, service, and appreciation. As organizations assist people who are undernourished, economically challenged or homeless, their brand becomes one of generosity and conscious service.

Advanced teachers remind us that money is inanimate. Money is a symbol. Money carries the energy that is assigned to it. Thus, money carries the energy of scarcity or abundance from people. People's lower mind projects fear and scarcity, while their higher mind projects abundance and peace. Steve D'Annunzio's *The Prosperity Paradigm* explains these themes in greater detail.

I redefine true wealth as *enrichment*. Abundance and prosperity exist on many levels. Abundance refers to lives rich with relationships, love, adequate finances, inner peace, and learning. The universe returns all the riches that you donate, tithe, and contribute as enrichment in your life.

When conscious beings share their abundance, the experience is rewarding. One of life's greatest joys can be to enrich the lives of people who may be less fortunate. As a guideline, ancient spiritual practices proposed that people tithe ten percent of their income to charity, ten percent to taxes and public services, and leave eighty percent for their families and loved ones.

Tithing is sacred service. Generosity reconnects your heart with the hearts of others and offers us the deepest meaning of community. Leaders and organizations that share their abundance, through contribution to others, enrich their own lives from within.

Principle **69**

Integrate the Feminine into Leadership

Know the male, yet keep the female;
receive the world in your arms.
—Tao Te Ching

Feminine energy, like love itself, is profoundly wise and powerful, yet nurturing and gentle. There is greater importance today for business leaders to truly embrace the nurturing nature of femininity. It provides balance in our leadership energy and business culture. Women have often been conspicuously absent from our corporate meritocracy until recent years. Femininity contributes the balanced energy of intuitive wisdom, whole-heartedness, nurturing, and inclusiveness.

The conscious leadership paradigm is yielding to a more inclusive, embracing approach that seeks to explore and assuage differences. Femininity translates increased context with a core under-standing of content. Feminine energy is vigilant in its softening of extreme positions. It seeks reconciliation and healing and is conciliatory rather than aggressive.

The feminine viewpoint works toward under-standing of differences and mitigating positions, and it engenders consensus from opposing parties. Like spirit, the feminine energy seeks peaceful resolution through grace. It is the energy of universal motherhood—perhaps the strongest love in the universe. Feminine consciousness deserves a respected place in leadership.

Principle 70

Live Your Soul Purpose

No one is where he is by accident, and chance plays no part in God's plan.
—*A Course in Miracles*

What am I doing to discover the unique thing that I do which is really a gift to the world?
—Steve D'Annunzio
Author of *The Prosperity Paradigm*

Every soul brings a unique gift, a contribution to the common good that reflects some aspect of the unity conscious-ness. When you accept the challenge to implement your soul's purpose, you will be moving from career to mission.
—Richard Barrett
Author of *Liberating the Corporate Soul*

In a life of purpose, we make a life worth living. We make a noteworthy contribution to the world where we find our own inner meaning. Our soul purpose is more of a destiny or contribution than a specific job or career path. Conscious leaders see their roles as contributors on a larger stage.

Soul purpose is the realm in which we find untiring interest, zeal, and joy. Purpose feeds us; it rejuvenates us. In this endeavor, we find self-restoring energy. Soul purpose is living a life of satisfying experience. Purpose gives people lives of vibrancy, filled with inspiration, enthusiasm, passion, optimism, and joy. Life becomes a journey of discovery. When we engage in activities related to our soul purpose, we derive immense satisfaction and an unquestioned sense of inner fulfillment from them.

When fully engaged, many artists, musical composers, teachers, and writers experience an "altered state" of effortless creativity. Time ceases to exist. Inspired activity of this kind is a sign that one is engaged in soul purpose. The energy and engagement are self-evident.

Swiss psychotherapist Carl Jung coined the psycho-spiritual phenomenon of *synchronicity*. He initially identified synchronicities as "the outer world's reflections of inner changes of consciousness."

Jung observed that when we pay attention to the voice of our soul, certain synchronicities effortlessly occur in our lives. He observed that when people live truly inspired lives propelled by a higher purpose for the greater good, they were met on their path with support and resources. Virtually everything they needed to fulfill their destiny simply showed up at the appropriate time. Jung discovered that it was not merely fortunate coincidences amid random circumstances. Many conclude that there are no chance events, that it is higher intention that generates an evolving synchronous creation. Synchronicity suggests what has always been part of a universal plan. We are all invited to participate and engage in the larger plan for the higher good of all. Conscious leaders embrace opportunities knowing that they are part of a greater whole.

The specifics of leaders' lives are part of the natural flow of experience. My soul purpose became easy to identify. Nothing gives me more pleasure than coaching, teaching, mentoring, guiding, and assisting others to foster their potential as leaders. Often, the greatest indication of finding one's soul purpose is the strong desire to share one's zeal and encouragement with others.

Finding one's soul purpose is not age specific. Leaders often experience life as a series of plateaus where they reinvent themselves at each level. Some may experience an inner awakening during midlife and completely change careers. Others experience a profound calling when being in the phenomenal presence of a great teacher or inspirational leader.

Whenever a profound soul purpose is found, great leaders and often great new organizations and causes are created.

Principle 71

Embrace the Impossible as Possible

Nothing is impossible; there are ways that lead to everything and if we had sufficient will, we should always have sufficient means. It is often merely for an excuse we say things are impossible.
—Francois La Rochefoucauld

Every generation that has gone before has stretched the upper limits of imagination. Just conceive how different life would be without electricity, radio, television, telephones, computers, the Internet, automobiles, and jet aircraft. An imaginative visionary brought each of those life-changing inventions to the world. These inventive leaders conceived these ideas in mind through higher inspiration and then manifested them in the physical realm.

In *The Last Word on Power*, Tracy Goss identifies a winning strategy that she suggests is literally encoded within leaders' makeup. She states, "Your winning strategy is not what you do. It is the source of what you do. It is the manifestation of who you are being." A winning strategy works up to a point; it is the human perspective of what can be. Leaders interpret what is possible through this paradigm and make incremental improvements.

Ms. Goss then describes *executive reinvention* as transitioning from the limitations of a winning strategy into an entirely new paradigm. The new paradigm creates an entirely new invented reality. Instead of looking at what is possible (through the eyes of a winning strategy), the new paradigm asks the leader to make possible the seemingly impossible. When leaders create a new imagined reality—envisioning what is beyond impediments or limitations—they make a declaration to manifest the impossible as possible. What had been perceived as impossible often becomes possible and becomes reality.

There are many examples throughout history. The Wright brothers envisioned, impossibly, a heavier-than-air machine that would fly. Gandhi envisioned the British relinquishing their hold on India and devoted his life to nonviolent response until that became reality. Electricity, the telephone, the automobile, and the personal computer seem mundanely ordinary today; however, they were revolutionary at the time of their introduction. They were once considered impossibilities.

Tracy Goss' ideas are countercultural. Executive reinvention propels the revolutionary idea that leaders are often capable of manifesting what is deemed as defying impossible odds, impossible stakes, beyond chance or probability. A created reality is most often limited by beliefs as to what is possible, *from the past.* Ordinarily, leaders manifest through the time-honored methods of incremental improvement. Making the impossible happen is the next level. The entire belief structure is challenged and then reinvented. Here, focused intention and relentless effort are aligned with advancing the possible.

With executive reinvention, the leader takes a defined stand that generates a unique certainty. But this is no ordinary stand, because it is without historical precedent, evidence, or proof. It is a commitment to take action, even if against the odds. This committed action creates a clearing in which the future can happen.

Unlike a goal, the realm of possibility is not a "go to" place from the present. It is an invented future to "come from" into the present. Since it is unrelated to the past, there is no conventional "in order to" component. There is no specified end result, success, or failure, only fulfilling a specified realm of possibility. Daunting to most leadership paradigms, there is no failure. Failure is irrelevant because declaration, stand, and effort still move the possibility forward.

Realization calls for leaders to be *executive catalysts. Leaders are the creators of the new reality, the next paradigm, and a new existence.* An entirely new frontier exists when leadership is reinvented in this way, causing the impossible to happen.

Principle 72

Let Go of Your Story

Who would you be without your story? You never know until you inquire. There is no story that is you or that leads to you. Every story leads away from you. You are what exists before all stories. You are what remains when the story is understood.
—Byron Katie
Author of *A Thousand Names for Joy*

Our personalities are the sum collection of our thoughts and feelings. People create stories about themselves based on their beliefs of who they are. People add all types of limitations and beliefs about who they cannot be into these stories as well.

As children, we received conditioning from our families of origin and from cultural systems into which we were born. We accumulated many perceptions, which became our closely held view of reality. Many self-concepts are formed from these sources, including limiting beliefs. Inaccurate perceptions form our story.

As adults transcend childhood beliefs, they are continually challenged to grow beyond early life limitations and to focus on creating new possibilities for themselves, entirely new ways of being. As people and leaders, we are called upon to challenge and transcend limiting beliefs. Earlier perceptions were put there to protect us. But from what? Is you story protecting you from the truth of who you are? Your magnificence is not your story.

During my graduate study in spiritual psychology, I received a supportive environment to inquire about my own perceptions of reality and to challenge my personal limiting beliefs. It didn't take long to discover that all limiting mental concepts are based on fear. For leaders and executives, transcending limiting beliefs has often called *reinvention*. Bringing out the true leader in you is often bringing out the authentic you. Your magnificence is already there, however, it may be clouded by limiting beliefs.

Byron Katie teaches a most effective way to inquire into our thoughts and examine our beliefs with understanding. Freedom from our story brings us inner peace. In her workshops, Katie instructs that thoughts are concepts that can become belief systems. As people believe these thoughts, the thinking becomes their perceived world. When people believe self-concepts that are not based in reality, they argue with reality and suffer as a result. People often hold beliefs regarding the way things "should be" that often are not aligned with "reality". That is where our story is created—in the mind—believing our story is the cause of all suffering. Through inquiry, we can find truth.

In her workshops, tapes, and books entitled *The Work*, Katie supportively urges people to examine those thoughts that cause them stress and suffering. These thoughts keep people small and captive within a story, which is based upon seeking identity and security. Katie encourages individuals to meet their thoughts with understanding; to seek the truth in the name of peace. The inquiry consists of four direct questions and turnarounds to inquire whether thoughts and beliefs are actually true. I have found no other system of inquiry as effective, straightforward, powerful, and understandable as *The Work*.

Through personal discovery, I have found that often my greatest learning begins with unlearning. I found it necessary to challenge conventional wisdom and discover my own truth. Most often, old conditioning was premised upon fears or weaknesses, never my strength, which is love and compassion.

In my personal experience, the greatest insight occurs when old limiting thoughts simply are no longer believed. They were just the story I told myself over and over, until I believed it. I actually believed the story was "me." The journey inward can only lead to one place— knowing the authentic self, the true source.

Challenging these old formative beliefs is not for the faint of heart. However, the most rewarding part of this life journey, for those willing to inquire, is to discover our authentic self, not the "version" called our *story*. There is an enormous difference between perception and truth. Are you ready to give up your story?

If your answer is yes, I welcome you to the journey of your lifetime. The gift of this journey is immeasurable.

For more information on The Work of Byron Katie, please go to her website www.thework.com .

Principle 73

Create Mindshift
through a Mastermind

Analyze the record of any person who has accumulated great fortune, and many of those who have accumulated modest fortunes, and you will find that they have either consciously or unconsciously employed the Master Mind principle.

—Napolean Hill
Author of *Think and Grow Rich*

A miracle is a change in perception.

—*A Course in Miracles*

The purpose of a mastermind group is to create *mind shift*, where the mind shifts above the current limit or perspective. Consciousness is like a ladder; *mind shift is a shift to higher consciousness*. Through mastermind, individuals tap into what has been called *infinite mind* or *creative mind*, the source. The source is the region where imagination and inspiration are accessed. As consciousness rises, reality changes. When our old paradigm is changed, a newly created experience is possible. The impossible becomes possible.

When a leader creates a mastermind, he or she attracts a group of dedicated, like-minded, and ideally like-hearted people whose sum is greater than the whole of the parts. Each participant is a champion of what the group hopes to create and what each individual hopes to discover within. Mastermind is more than team building; it is the art form of leadership creation.

Masterminding creates a special environment for creation and reinvention. Mastermind is a judgment-free place; it is a bias-free place; it is a worry-free place. Participants receive unparalleled encourage-ment to ask for their new vision, often their lifetime dream. Each individual's life aspirations and advancement intentions become supported in manifold ways. Participants may mentor one another. Each person is challenged, through inquiry, to see new possibilities and potential. The group motivates and encourages the collective body to give a voice to their dream.

Each participant then forms a vision of what could be, to take action, and to create a life of empowered choice, not deferral or incremental improvement. Each participant is invited to give birth to a new paradigm, a life realization. The process embraces expanding perspectives, stretching boundaries, transcending apparent limits, and envisioning new ways of being.

In my own mastermind group, there is extraordinary connection. We are each tapped in to something greater than ourselves. All sense of individual isolation or false identity vanishes. We have received an exceptional opportunity, supported by the group, to create our transition to the next level and beyond. That transition has no limits other than our own. Besides the group process, we incorporate selected readings from industry leaders, respected coaches and consultants, and reinvention professionals. The sessions are very empowering. However, it is the personal process of inquiry and contemplation between the sessions that produces our growth and enrichment. We are stretching our limits and we are expanding our lives.

I wholeheartedly encourage interested leaders to create a mastermind group with his/her own leadership team, with other business leaders or leaders in the community. The mastermind process is extraordinarily gratifying and the results can be phenomenal. In mastermind, the mind power, the heart power, the life power, and the soul power of human beings are conjoined; they work together for the greater good. Masterminding is that rarified "all for one and one for all."

Principle 74

Awaken to Conscious Purpose

Self Concept is Destiny.
> —Lindsay Brady, Hypnotherapist

Security is mostly superstition. Life is either a daring adventure or nothing.
> —Helen Keller

The power center for ... renewed leadership for the common good lies in the personal resilience of the mature contingents who will dominate American life for at least the next quarter century.... each of us will gain most when we commit ourselves to the transformation of our common consciousness.
> —Frederic M. Hudson
> Author of *The Adult Years*

The integration of who we are with what we do is one of the greatest joys of life. We are all challenged to discover and create the specific and unique way we are going to work and be all we are called to do.

I spent many years seeking meaning and expression through my work, my calling, and my spiritual practice. In discerning my purpose, my greatest personal discovery was that life itself is a journey whose purpose is to transcend fear, a continual opening to change, expansion, and courage. The journey involves awakening to a universal presence of connection to others, characterized by compassion and contribution. Advanced leadership stirs such an awakening. A number of great teachers and authors have described our journey as climbing a *spiritual ladder* where fear-based energy is near the bottom and love-based energy at the top. Fear is a reactive energy of blame, resistance, and judgment. Loving essence is expansive, proactive, creative, and inclusive of all.

Most startling of all, some of my wisest teachers have urged me to return to a childlike nature of joy and discovery, living in the present moment. I can assure you that joy and discovery were conspicuously missing from many of my adult years and career progressions. I existed in an imagined future.

Somehow, most of us seem to lose that childlike fascination as young adults. Why? First, we become conditioned to seek approval and appreciation of others, preoccupied with how we are perceived. That can lead to needing to win over others. Second, the underlying dominant human thought system is focused on two themes: our *identity* and our *security* (comfort and safety). There is a belief in the lower mind that we exist as a physical body. It's a leftover part of our reptilian, survival-based brain.

This predominant thought system if unchecked can leave us in a state of almost-constant anxiety, doubt, and fear. The inner script states that "there will never be enough" whether it is addressing money, love or whatever. This so-called *survival mentality* cannot lead to peace.

Survival is a projection, where happiness is based upon external events, which cannot be controlled. Thus, survival mentality projects scarcity into an imagined future, whether about food, shelter, health, money, or well-being. This universal human paradigm most often sees life through the filter of how life "should be" rather than appreciating "what is" through the perspective of gratitude. The majority of people think that there *shouldn't* be problems; something is *wrong* when the world presents problems. Often the "problem" with a problem is all of the negative emotion invested in the concept. Challenges do happen.

Early in this book, I defined leadership as a discipline, a process. I believe a defining process of leadership is the ascent to living with *conscious purpose*, centered in contribution and service to others. Contribution leads us away from what "should be" to what "can be." Such leadership creates a meaningful, fulfilling life for us. Contribution and conscious purpose remove us from the perception of feeling isolated to a state of intimate connection with others. It is impossible to feel anxious, depressed or insecure when we are serving others. When we demonstrate compassion and understanding for others, our personal insecurity vanishes.

Conscious purpose constitutes an advanced leadership skill because transcending fear is also surrendering the illusion of control. Things only become an issue when we are outside the *now*. Worry is an imagined future; leadership involves a created future. Life presents events, circumstances, and opportunities. Within our defined *conscious purpose*, we choose our intention, attitude, and responses to them. We become more interested in a life of creating something, rather than a life of preventing something. With conscious purpose, we give up the human paradigm of how life "should be" and move forward into how life "can be."

The ascent into leadership is a life's learning, journeying beyond limitation and fear. While challenging and difficult at times, I believe that the ascent through fear is the most profound, exciting lesson of all. By transcending fear we experience freedom, the end of personal suffering. Beyond fear is truth and truth will set us free.

Committing to purpose and the fearless joy of living are consummate skills of conscious leadership. Why? When we journey past fear, we are free. Freedom is the state of being fearless, where we are the abundance of love. That is when our joy and discovery are re-experienced. We were asleep, but then we awakened. Experientially, a loving consciousness is the ultimate leadership competency.

Principle 75

Live from a Level of Conscious Leadership

Conscious leadership is an outgrowth of leaders' beliefs and personal levels of learning maturity and compassion. Corporate transformation consultant Richard Barrett created this powerful leadership model, which follows, based upon Abraham Maslow's *The Hierarchy of Human Needs*.

The levels correlate to the human-maturation process and include life-stage progressions. People are influenced and affected by their family of origin, cultural identification, education, career, and life choices. People dispel ego, gain wisdom, and develop consciousness.

The three lower levels are highly imbued with a self-based construct.

The first three levels contain a "shadow." Shadow exists where excessive focus or enforced implementation of that level is practiced, a type of coercion. That type of application is manipulative rather than empowering or liberating.

The upper four levels are characterized by an increasing focus on empathy, service, compassion, inclusiveness, and contribution for others in an expanding dynamic of the company being envisioned as a conscious community.

The Seven Levels of Leadership Consciousness

Level One: The Crisis Manager

An intense focus on profit and survival exists on this level. Leaders function as firefighters and are prone to being reactive, rather than proactive. Level One leaders view work as a struggle and view financial gain as a result of a finite amount of exploitation and control. A fledgling business often has limited financial reserves at inception. Financial constraints may affect the level of service external clients receive and may also strain the resources and energy of internal members.

Level Two: The Relationship Director

The core focus on this level of relatedness involves serving the corporate needs. Relationships are viewed as serving the mission for profit and growth. Little time or resources are allocated for personal training and development to keep pace with the organizations' growth. Leaders are in a state of constant "doing." The focus involves serving the external clients. Little refueling or recharging exists for the internal producers. Often blame and manipulation occur as resources strain to accommodate growth and customer service. Results and profit are all-important. Employees are placed behind profit and external customers, and long-term morale suffers.

Level Three: The Organizer/Director

Efficiency, productivity, technology, systems, and process are the focus at this level. Leaders place great emphasis on profit margins and service delivery. Training and mentoring of employees are a lower priority. Bureaucracy and internal complacency abide because systems are favored over people. Employees' creativity is not promulgated or given a place of priority in the focus upon systems, process, and production.

Level Four: The Influencer /Facilitator

This transformational level serves as a gateway to the upper levels. Innovation and continuous renewal are emphasized. Leaders rethink, plan, reinvent system, and retool through process improvement. Independent creativity and the contribution of individual employees are encouraged and valued. True team building and authentic delegation and ownership occur. No predominant shadow exists at this level.

At Levels Five through Seven, *servant leaders* become the dominant leader paradigm within the construct.

Level Five: The Inspiring Integrator

Corporate community resides at this level. Vibrant and pervasive positive corporate culture thrives within the business model and systems. Mission and vision are imbued with shared core values. They are integral creeds, rather than brochure verbiage. Cultural cohesion, corporate cooperation, and creativity are evident in all company functions. These soft-side dynamics begin to propel measurable contributions to productivity, profitability, and efficiency. People and organizational morale levels are high and continuous.

Level Six: The Partner/Mentor

Collaboration and outreach with customers, stakeholders, and local and regional community occur at this level. The firm and members of its territory are viewed as strategic allies. Employee empowerment, community advocacy, and environmental stewardship are integral parts of the organization's fabric and ethical soundness. Community contribution in time and money are valued and viewed as strategic partners.

Level Seven: The Visionary/ Wisdom Leader

Service to the whole community, the nation, the global village, and the environment becomes central in the firm's progression and growth. The focus is leaders create and co-create with compassion and vision with and for the global community. A long-term perspective, concern for the global population, and a sense of moral purpose abound. As these values embody the core essence of leadership, all leaders, people, and the planet prosper.

Innovative, compassionate, conscious leaders who serve on the global level are welcome and needed to create organizations whose missions and purpose benefit the good of all. The global village calls for a new order of leaders. The level Five, Six and Seven Leaders are the new order of conscious leaders needed for the 21st Century.

Epilogue

The 21st Century is calling out for a new order of leader. That leader is the conscious leader who embraces the highest good of the organization, all of its stakeholders, and the greater community at large. That leader is a spiritual, ethical being who communicates artfully from an authentic center. That leader is a compassionate creator.

What you have before you today is a thorough collection of what I consider the highly learnable skills of conscious leadership. Each of us is born with intrinsic talent; the remainder is learned and developed. The Principles are actually practices that can be embraced by anyone who desires to transform their leadership skills from within. Please use this text as a handbook and a reference guide.

Please remember, these principles were written to awaken the leadership skills that already dwell within you.

With blessings and joy for your leadership journey,
Michael Schantz
Los Angeles, CA
January 2008

Recommended Readings
on Consciousness and Leadership

1. *Getting Things Done* — David Allen
2. *Leadership and Self-Deception* — The Arbinger Institute
3. *The Prosperity Paradigm* — Steve D'Annunzio
4. *Love and Profit* — James A. Autry
5. *A Guide to Liberating Your Soul* — Richard Barrett
6. *Liberating the Corporate Soul* — Richard Barrett
7. *Self-Esteem at Work* — Nathaniel Branden
8. *Feeling Good* — David D. Burns, M.D
9. *100 Ways to Motivate Others* — Steve Chandler
10. *100 Ways to Create Wealth* — Steve Chandler
11. *The Joy of Selling* — Steve Chandler
12. *Ten Commitments to Your Success* — Steve Chandler
13. *The Game of Work* — Charles Coonradt
14. *Principle-Centered Leadership* — Stephen R. Covey
15. *(Great) Employees Only* — Dale Dauten
16. *The Gifted Boss* — Dale Dauten
17. *The Power of Intention* — Wayne W. Dyer, Ph.D.
18. *The Radical Leap* — Steve Farber
19. *The Power of Kindness* — Pierro Ferucci
20. *The Sermon on the Mount* — Emmett Fox
21. *A Reinvention of Work* — Matthew Fox
22. *The Last Word on Power* — Tracy Goss
23. *Mindful Loving* — Henry Grayson, Ph.D.
24. *The Power of Servant Leadership* — Robert K. Greenleaf
25. *Spirituality in the Workplace* — William A. Guillory
26. *Power versus Force* — David R. Hawkins, M.D.
27. *Conscious Loving* — Gay & Kathlyn Hendricks
28. *Forgiveness, the Greatest Healer* — Gerald G. Jampolsky, M.D
29. *Loving What Is* — Byron Katie
30. *Conscious Leadership* — Fred Kofman

31. *Appreciative Inquiry*   Little Books
32. *The Relationship Handbook*   George H. Pransky, Ph.D
33. *The Power of Full Engagement*   Jim Loehr
                                      and Tony Schwartz
34. *A New Earth*   Eckhardt Tolle
35. *Investment Leadership*   Jim Ware
36. *Journey of the Heart*   John Welwood, Ph.D.
37. *The Eye of Spirit*   Ken Wilber

About the Author

The author, Michael Schantz, has spent the past twenty-five years working within the financial services industry for major Fortune 500 companies. He holds his M.B.A. from The American University and earned his Masters degree in Psychology from the University of Santa Monica, known for its experiential programs in spirituality, healing, and leadership.

Michael has developed a lifelong interest in human potential, life purpose, the mind, human motivation, and the development of leadership as a learned discipline. During the 1980s and 1990s, Michael observed, firsthand, the dramatic changes that occurred within many companies. Sweeping changes occurred with the advent of technology, downsizing, and the globalization of international market economies. He noted that the effect on workers was adaptive, dramatic, and impacting. With those dramatic changes facing leaders, he queried how the role of managers and leaders would rapidly evolve with changing professional roles, work production, plus maintaining balance in their personal lives.

Besides his career in financial services, Michael is a life life coach and executive mentor in Los Angeles, California. He may be reached at mschantz@sbcglobal.net .

Great Books For Success and Leadership

Send indicated books to:

Name _____

Address_____

City _____State_____Zip_____

Phone _____Fax_____Cell _____

E-Mail _____

Payment by check /_/ or credit card /_/ *(All major credit cards are accepted.)*

Name on card _____

Card Number_____

Exp. Date _____ Last 3-Digit number on back of card _____

Qty.

75 Principles of Conscious Leadership
by Michael Schantz . . . .$14.95 _____

100 Ways to Create Wealth
by Steve Chandler & Sam Beckford . . . .$24.95 _____

The Joy of Selling
by Steve Chandler . . . .$11.95 _____

Customer Astonishment: 10 Secrets to World-Class Customer Care
by Darby Checketts. . . . .$14.95 _____

The Chic Entrepreneur: Put Your Business in Higher Heels
by Elizabeth Gordon . . . .$12.95 _____

Handling Employment for Bosses and Supervisors
by Geoffrey Hopper . . . .$19.95 _____

How Bad Do You Really Want It?
by Tom Massey . . . .$19.95 _____

Quantity of Books ordered:_____ Total: _____

Note: Shipping is $3.50 1st book + $1 for each additional book. Postage_____

FINAL TOTAL ENCLOSED:$_____

Visit our website—www.rdrpublishers.com—for more great titles.